The Ch~ ~e
Early ~ons

~ *Brut y Bryttaniait* ~

according to
Jesus College MS LXI

An annotated translation
by
Bill Cooper

Copyright 2018 Dr Wm R Cooper
ISBN 978-1-9996090-0-9

About the Author

Bill Cooper is a Vice President and Trustee of the Creation Science Movement in England. He also serves as Adjunct Professor of Providential History and Apologetics on the Master Faculty at the Institute for Creation Research School of Biblical Apologetics.

He is the author of *After the Flood* (1995); *Paley's Watchmaker* (1997); *William Tyndale's 1526 New Testament* (old spelling ed. British Library. 2000); *The Wycliffe New Testament of 1388* (British Library. 2002); *The Authenticity of the Book of Genesis* (CSM. 2012); *The Authenticity of the Book of Daniel* (2012); *The Authenticity of the Book of Jonah* (2012); *The Authenticity of the Book of Esther* (2012); *The Chronicle of the Early Britons* (2012); *Old Light on the Roman Church* (2012); *The Authenticity of the New Testament Part 1: The Gospels* (2013); *The Authenticity of the New Testament Part 2: Acts, The Epistles and Revelation* (2013); *The Authenticity of the Book of Joshua* (2015); *The Authenticity of the Book of Judges* (2015); *The Forging of Codex Sinaiticus* (2016); and *New Testament Fragments amongst the Dead Sea Scrolls* (2017). He has also authored numerous technical articles on Creationism, Palaeo-anthropology, Bible Apologetics, the Reformation and the History of the English Bible.

Graduating with Honours at Kingston University (England), he went on to obtain both his PhD and ThD from Emmanuel College of Christian Studies (Springdale, Arkansas). He lives in England, is married to Eileen (for more than 45 years now), has two daughters, numerous foster children, four fine grandsons and a granddaughter.

Acknowledgements

My thanks must go to the Principal and Fellows of Jesus College, Oxford, for their kind permission to translate Jesus College MS LXI, and to publish that translation; with special thanks to D A Rees, the archivist at the College; to Ellis Evans, Professor of Celtic Studies at Jesus, who scrutinized the translation; and last but by no means least, to Mike Gascoigne for kindly formatting the footnotes.

Design and illustration

Text composition and cover design by Kevin Tuck. The front cover includes a detail from an illustration in *The Book of Kells* and a composite image of a mediaeval text; both are in the public domain. The title font is Cardinal, by kind permission of Dieter Steffmann.

Introduction

There lies in an Oxford library a certain old and jaded manuscript. It is written in medieval Welsh in an informal cursive hand, and is a 15th-century copy of a 12th-century original (now lost). Its shelfmark today is Jesus College MS LXI, but that has not always been its name. For some considerable time it went under the far more evocative name of the Tysilio Chronicle, and earlier this century a certain archaeologist made the following observation concerning it. The year was 1917, the archaeologist was Flinders Petrie, and his observation was that this manuscript was being unaccountably neglected by the scholars of his day. It was, he pointed out, perhaps the best representative of an entire group of chronicles in which are preserved certain important aspects of early British history, aspects that were not finding their way into the published notices of those whose disciplines embraced this period.

After all, he opined, it is not as if this chronicle poses any threat or particular challenge to the accepted wisdom of the day. On the contrary, it illuminates parts of early British history that are otherwise obscure, and in one or two places sheds light where before there was only complete and utter darkness. So exactly why this chronicle was so neglected in Flinders Petrie's day, and indeed why it continues to be omitted from any serious discussion more than 100 years on, is one of those strange imponderables of life.

Doubtless there are a thousand reasons why historians pay no great heed to this ancient record, but that is no sufficient cause why it should go unread at all. Whether this passage or that is historically reliable or no are matters for scholars to wrangle over, and this they may do to their hearts' content. Indeed, certain points of this chronicle's historicity are considered in the appropriate chapters of *After the Flood* (see Appendix II). But, degrees of historicity or otherwise notwithstanding, the most important consideration of all is that our ancient forebears believed it to be a true and honest account. This is how they saw their world and the past which led them to it, and this is the literary heritage that they have taken such pains to pass down to us. For that reason alone, their work should be read and admired – yes, and studied too – and towards that end the following translation of the manuscript has been made.

I see no good reason why these ancient voices should be consigned to such oblivion when they have such a rich story to tell – a tale which weaves a veritable tapestry of kings and battles, triumphs and disasters, about which not one of us has heard at our school desks and which have waited many centuries to be told. It is a history that begins with the Fall of Troy. It tells of fortune and cunning, of heroism and cowardice, of chivalry and murder, of loyalty and betrayal. It concerns the birth of a people, the settling of an island, the succession of their kings, and the timely correction of their sins under the chastising hand of God. We hear of Romans and Saxons, of Picts, Scots and Irish, of witchery and plague, of idleness and plenty, invasion and security. Traitors, kings and tyrants walk side by side over its pages, and there can be few accounts from any age or nation that can come near to challenging this ancient chronicle either for high drama or the sheer power of its narrative.

For the reader or student who wishes to delve further into the chronicle, there are copious footnotes added which deal with points of linguistic, historical, geographical and other concerns. Some of these notes will answer questions, whilst others, it is greatly hoped, will raise them. Either way, interest and inquiry will be stimulated towards a most important yet too little known aspect of our literary heritage, and if the present translation contributes something at least towards that end, then I shall consider its job well done.

Bill Cooper

Translator's Note

Welsh texts of any century present the English translator with a problem or two concerning personal and place names, and there are hundreds of these in the chronicle that we are about to read. At the best of times, English readers find Welsh names impossibly difficult to pronounce, and the immediate task is always to render the names so that the English reader will not constantly trip over them. In my own attempt to solve the problem, I came to admire the ingenuity of Geoffrey of Monmouth who made a Latin version of the same chronicle at Oxford in the year 1136.

Now, it is exceedingly rare these days to find even grudging praise being offered to Geoffrey, yet I do not hesitate to pay him the present compliment at least, for Geoffrey's achievement was to Latinize the Welsh names in such a way as to make them pronounceable to his own readers of the early 12th century, and so successful were his efforts that I make no apology whatever for borrowing many of his renderings. After all, the problem is exactly the same today as it was in his time.

What, for example, would a modern English reader make of the name *Gwrvyw*? Like his 12th-century Latin-reading counterpart, he would baulk at guessing its pronunciation. That alone would greatly spoil his reading, and there is a whole sea of such names for him to wade through. But Geoffrey solved the problem beautifully in this case with the rendering *Gorboduc*. This I have shamelessly borrowed.

Here and there, however, I did find it expedient to abandon even Geoffrey's ingenious renderings, for he would sometimes give a Latin rendering which was as difficult to pronounce as the Welsh. For example, he takes the Welsh *Gwychlan* and turns it bravely into *Ginchtalacus*. As the subject who owned this name was a Dane, I have abandoned Geoffrey here altogether and simply given the original Danish form, which is *Guthlac*. This and similar cases should present the modern reader with no difficulty at all.

Place names were much easier to deal with, for where these can be identified I have simply given their modern forms. *Kaer Benhwylgoed*, for example, is present-day Exeter; *Kaer Gradawc* is Salisbury; *Kaer Vynnydd y Paladr* is likewise Shaftesbury. Each modern place name, however, is accompanied on its first appearance by a footnote which supplies the original Welsh reading.

Finally, where, for the sake of intelligibility, I have had to add English words where no Welsh original exists, I have followed the time-honoured convention of enclosing them within square parentheses [ ]. And where italicized proper names appear, these are given in place of the inordinate number of pronouns that litter the text, and which would otherwise have rendered obscure many parts of the narrative. After all, it helps to know just who is doing the talking or the deed!

Bill Cooper

Abbreviations

Throughout the footnotes only two abbreviations are used. The first, LXI, refers to *Jesus College MS LXI*, of which this present work is a translation; whilst the second, GoM, refers to Geoffrey of Monmouth's *Historia Regum Britanniae*, a Latin version of the chronicle which bears repeated comparison with the Jesus College manuscript. The works of all other authors whose names alone appear in the footnotes, are given in the Bibliography.

The Chronicle of the Early Britons

Early Britons

~ Brut y Bryttaniait ~

[The Chronicle of the Early Britons]
[Prologue] [1]

Britain, the fairest of islands, whose name of old was Albion,[2] which lies in the Western Ocean twixt Gaul[3] and Ireland,[4] is eight hundred miles in length and two hundred broad, supplying the needs of its people with unending bounty. Its wide plains and rolling hills fill the land, and into its harbours flow the goods of many nations. It has forests and woods wherein are found all manner of creatures and wild beasts, and bees gather nectar from its flowers. It has beautiful meadows at the foot of rugged mountains, and pure clean springs with lakes and rivers teeming with all manner of fish. There are three great rivers:[5] the Thames,[6] the Humber,[7] and the Severn,[8] and these embrace the island like three great arms, along them being carried the trade and produce of lands across the seas.[9]

In ancient times there beautified the land three and thirty great and noble cities,[10] of which some are now desolate, their walls cast down. But others are still lived in, and contain sacred places within them for the worship of God. And the land is now inhabited by five peoples:[11] the Britons,[12] the Normans,[13] the Saxons,[14] the Picts,[15] and the Scots.[16] And of all these peoples, it is the Britons

---

1) Prologues somewhat similar to this are found in Gildas, Bede, the Anglo-Saxon Chronicle, GoM and elsewhere. Their usage suggests that they were intended for a wide international readership, describing Britain for those who were unfamiliar with the country.
2) LXI = *y wen ynys* - lit. the White Island.
3) LXI = *ffraink*. The land of the Franks, more properly Gaul.
4) LXI = *iwerddon*.
5) As in GoM, but Gildas gives two rivers, omitting the Humber. Bede omits all three, which at least rules out copying or interdependency between them.
6) LXI = *temys*. Modern Welsh has Tafwys.
7) LXI = *hymyr*.
8) LXI = *hafrenn*.
9) Gildas (chap. 3 - see Bibliography) has: "...[two] arms of the sea along which luxuries from overseas used to be brought by ship." It is interesting that Gildas, in the 6th century, should use the past tense where the earlier source for the chronicle uses the present.
10) GoM gives twenty-eight cities, as do Gildas and Bede, the latter of whom stresses that this was in "olden times" by AD 730.
11) Curiously, Bede omits the Saxons.
12) LXI = *bryttanniait*.
13) LXI = *normaniaid*.
14) LXI = *ssaesson*. A more modern form of the name is to be seen in the Scots *sassenach*, a disdainful term for the English, as is the modern Welsh, *Saesneg*.
15) LXI = *ffichtiait*.
16) LXI = *yssgottiaid*.

who were its first inhabitants and who once filled the land from the Channel[17] to the Irish Sea - until, that is, the judgment of God fell upon them for their iniquities, which we shall presently set forth.

And with this ends the Prologue of Aeneas, [surnamed] Whiteshield.[18]

Once the city [of Troy][19] had fallen, Aeneas[20] fled, and Ascanius[21] his son also, and they arrived in ships in that part of Italy[22] called nowadays the land of Rome.[23] And in those days, Latinus[24] was king of Italy, and he welcomed Aeneas with honour. Then, once Aeneas had done battle with Turnus,[25] the king of the Rutuli,[26] who was killed by Aeneas, Ascanius, [the son of Aeneas], wedded Lavinia, the daughter of Latinus. Then, after Aeneas, Ascanius [himself] became a great man, and when Ascanius was raised to the kingdom

---

17) The English Channel. LXI gives *mor rrydd*, which, as Griscom points out (p. 537), more properly translates as the Sea of the Ruteni (OFr. *Rudein*), the Ruteni inhabiting southern Gaul in Roman times. The ancient form *mor rrydd* indicates the great antiquity of some of the material in LXI's prologue. The modern Welsh form of its name is *Mor Udd*.

18) LXI = *Eneas yssgwyddwyn*. Aeneas White-shoulder would perhaps be more accurate. Was it the nickname (or *nom de plume*) of the 12th-century scholar who added this prologue to the chronicle - Caradoc of Llancarfan perhaps (see note 572), himself a Cistercian (White) monk and continuator of the *Brut y Tywysogyon* (Chronicle of the Princes)? The name occurs only once more in the chronicle when Kasswallon reminds Julius Caesar that *Eneas yssgwyddwyn* was the common ancestor of both the Romans and Britons.

19) The name of Troy does not appear here in the original (LXI). Its absence suggests that the name had appeared in a preceding passage, which in turn suggests that the very beginning of the original source document was missing when this Welsh translation was made in the mid-12th century.

20) LXI = *eneas*.

21) As in GoM (1:3). LXI = *essgannys*. Livy (p. 36) agrees that Ascanius married Lavinia, but adds that he founded the ancient city of Lavinium, so named in her honour, and then founded Alba Longa.

22) LXI = *eidial*.

23) LXI = *rryfain*.

24) LXI = *lattynis*, the eponymous founder of the Latin race. Such an attribution is not that unlikely. America, arguably the greatest nation on earth today, is named after the Portugese navigator, Amerigo Vespucci. Rhodesia is so named from Cecil Rhodes, and so on.

25) LXI = *tyrrv*. Turnus is also mentioned in Livy (p. 36). Livy, however, has Turnus surviving the battle and seeking help from the Etruscan prince Mezentius. The discrepancy demonstrates that LXI and GoM are no mere rehashes of Livy, whose work, in any case, was not available in 12th-century England.

26) LXI = *yttyl*. The Rutuli are also known from Livy. In 510 BC, they were conquered by Tarquin of Rome. They last appear in ca. 440 BC, after which date they slide into obscurity.

he founded a city on the banks of the river Tiber.[27] And in that place, a son was born to him named Silvius,[28] and he, Silvius, seduced his [own] niece and lay with her privily, getting her with child. And after Ascanius, his father, had heard of it, he commanded the wise men to tell him with whom the lass had lain. And after they perceived the matter and were sure of it, they said that the lass was carrying a son who would cause the deaths of his [own] father and mother, but after a time of exile and wandering through many lands, he would achieve great honour. Nor did the wise men deceive him, [for] when the lass's time had come to deliver the child, she died in her bed. And thus he, her son, killed his mother.

And the lad was called Brutus,[29] and he was given out to be fostered. And when he reached his fifteenth year, he was one day following his [natural] father out hunting. And behold, a great stag ran past, and Brutus drew back his bow and shot at the stag, but he struck his father in the breast with the arrow and he, his father, died. And so he killed his father also.

And for the death of Silvius, the men of Italy banished Brutus from the land, because it would be impious to have as king over them one who had committed such an outrageous deed as killing his [own] mother and father. And after his banishment [was pronounced], he, Brutus, travelled as far as Greece,[30] and [there] he saw the children of the sons of Helenus,[31] the son of Priam,[32] heirs of Troy,[33] [living] in slavery under Pandrasus,[34] king of Greece. For after the fall of Troy, Pyrrhus,[35] the son of Achilles,[36] in vengeance for his father's death, had for a long time held this people captive under him in slavery. When Brutus discovered that they were his own people, he remained with them. Then, once Brutus and they became acquainted with one another, the kings and princes bestowed [upon him] their acclaim because of his dignity and bearing, his courage and generosity, his skill in war, and his fame. Amongst the wise, he was

---

27) LXI = taiberys. More anciently known as the Albula, the Tiber formed the boundary between the Latins and the Etruscans (Livy, p. 37). It was said to have gained its later name from one Tiberinus who drowned in its waters.
28) LXI = ssylhys.
29) LXI = bryttys.
30) LXI = groec.
31) LXI = Elenys.
32) LXI = Priaf.
33) LXI = troyaf.
34) LXI = Pandrassys. Derived, perhaps, from pan Doris, i.e. the king of all Dorians. The period, 12th - 11th centuries BC, would be right for such a title.
35) LXI = Pyrr.
36) LXI = Achilarwy.

the wisest, and amongst the warriors [he was] the bravest. And whatever he possessed, whether it was of gold or silver, horses or raiment, he would apportion [them] amongst his closest friends as well as any other who would receive them of him. And so, after his renown had travelled throughout [all] the lands of Greece, and everyone of the House of Troy had come to him [even] from as far as the outer limits of Greece, they implored him to be prince over them and deliver them from their captivity. And they said to him that this would be as nothing for him to do, for enough of them were there to number seven thousand warriors. Moreover they said [among themselves]: "This young man, the most noble in Greece on his father's side, and [that of] his mother [who was] born of the lineage of Troy, looks to us in the hope of winning from us our strength and support. This is why the men of this land, along with his brother on his father's side, war against him. It is because [both] his mother and father are of Greek blood. [But] there is also bad blood between them because his father bequeathed three more castles to him, Brutus, when he died, than he left to his brother. And the Greeks hope to take them from him because of his mother's Trojan descent, by allying themselves with his brother against him!" And when Brutus had seen [for himself] the great multitude of them, and the castles fortified and made ready for him, it was a light matter to accede [to their wishes] and take upon himself the leading [of the people]. And once Brutus had been raised to be prince of the people of Troy, he fortified the castles of Asaracus,[37] and filled them with men, weapons and provisions. And when he had done this, [both] he and Asaracus, taking their armies and provisions with them, set out for the depths of the thick forests to which they retreated.

And then Brutus sent a message to Pandrasus, king of Greece, saying this: "Brutus, prince of the Trojan armies and people, sends this message to Pandrasus, king of Greece, saying to him that it is unworthy of him to hold in slavery a royal people of the lineage of Dardanus,[38] nor, for their nobility, to oppress them more than they deserve. Therefore Brutus tells him that they deem it better by far to live in the forests and to eat raw meat and grass with freedom, than [to dwell] amidst feasting and luxury as slaves. And if this provokes your pride against them as their lord and master, rather than war against them you ought to pardon them, for both nature and duty decree that every slave should seek to recover his ancient dignity and freedom. We therefore seek your sufferance and leave, that with freedom we might dwell in the forests to which

---

37) LXI = *Assarakys*.
38) LXI = *dardar*, the eponymous founder of the Biblical *Dodanim* (Gen. 10:4), whom the Greeks knew as the *Dardani*, i.e. the Dardanians of Asia Minor who gave their name in turn to the Dardanelles. The Egyptians knew them as the *drdny*, the allies of the Hittites at the Battle of Kadesh.

we have fled. Or if that cannot be, then allow us to find in other lands an habitation free from slavery!" And when Pandrasus understood the substance of the message, he wondered greatly that such a demand should be sent to him. And straightway he summoned his council before him, and this was its counsel to him - to muster a great army and pursue them into the forests. And as they, the Greeks, passed by under the castle called Thesprotikon,[39] Brutus fell upon them suddenly with three thousand warriors. And he caught them unarmed and wrought great destruction amongst them. And straightway they fled in disgrace - with their king in the lead! And they fled towards the river Acheron,[40] and such was their panic and dread of Brutus that some of them drowned, some were slain on the riverbank, and the remainder fled [the scene]. And thus he, Brutus, defeated them.

And when he saw this, Antigonus,[41] the brother of Pandrasus, was greatly saddened. He summoned his comrades, mustering them together, and attacked the men of Troy, thinking it better to die with honour than to live in shame. And he exhorted his soldiers to fight manfully. Then he signalled the attack and himself lent a hand in the fighting. But it availed him nothing, for Brutus and his soldiers had [the better] arms, whilst they, the Greeks, were unprepared, [having had] no time to put on their armour. And thus Brutus soon vanquished them, and took Antigonus, the king's brother, captive. Then Brutus fortified the castle of Asaracus, and manned it with six hundred warriors, and [together] with his army went back to the forest where they lived.

Pandrasus, alarmed at his [own] flight and by the capture of his brother, mustered as many of his soldiers as had escaped, and the following day laid siege to the castle. For he thought that Brutus was inside with his brother and all the other prisoners. And when he had come there, he assigned divisions of his army around the castle, the greater part of them to watch the gates that none might come out, another part to divert the castle's water supply, and the third part to construct [siege] engines in order to breach [and demolish the walls].

And according to the king's command, each made the best device he could. And when nightfall came upon them, he selected the fittest men to besiege the castle so that those who were exhausted might sleep, before Brutus and his army should fall upon them a second time. And the castellans fought against them

---

39) LXI = *Yssbaradings*. GoM gives *Sparatinum*. Both are derived from Thesprotia, an area on the western coast of Greece. The name is represented in the modern town of Thesprotikon.

40) LXI = *Ystalon*. GoM has *Akalon*, both versions seemingly corruptions of Acheron, a river of Thesprotia.

41) LXI = *Antigonys*.

heroically, shooting [arrows] and catapulting Greek Fire[42] upon them, and in diverse ways trying to drive them away from the wall.

And when they, the Greeks, had placed their [siege] engines against [the wall] and began to undermine it, the defenders poured Greek Fire and boiling water on their heads, and drove them from the [castle] wall. Then, when they were exhausted by their labours for want of sleep at night and through hunger and thirst, they, the Trojans, despatched runners to Brutus [to ask] for reinforcements, lest they be compelled to surrender the castle.

And when Brutus heard [their message] he was grieved, for he knew not how he could help them, as he had no sufficient army to openly do battle against the Greeks. Therefore he decided to wage a night attack against them, slay the sentries and fall upon the Greeks whilst they slept. But he knew that he could not do this without the help of the Greeks [themselves]. So he summoned Anacletus[43] before him, who was a friend of Antigonus, unsheathed his sword, held him tightly, and spoke to him in this manner: "Behold, young man, here is your death unless you faithfully perform the matter that I require of you. Tonight I shall attack the Greeks, but I require you to mislead them thus so that my way shall be unimpeded. Approach their sentries and tell them that you and Antigonus have broken out of my prison, and that you have left him in a wooded vale where he still is, by reason of the heavy irons that are laid upon him. And beseech them to accompany you back and bring him in. Do this, and I shall have my pleasure of them."

And when Anacletus beheld Brutus threatening him with death, he swore to be true to Brutus provided that Antigonus should [indeed] accompany him. And so they approached the Greeks. And when he, Anacletus, reached the sentries, they surrounded him and questioned him whether he had come to entrap them. "Indeed, no!" [he said]. "But I have borne Antigonus upon my back by stealth from Brutus' dungeon, and I left him concealed amongst the thorns and thistles in the valley below. Therefore make haste and help me fetch him." But they hesitated to accompany him for fear of betrayal, when one of them who knew him said that he spoke the truth. Then, in close formation, the sentries went with him to where he said Antigonus was. And Brutus fell upon them and slew them all. And then they, the Trojans, marched in order until they reached the midst of the [Greek] army. And they all were silent until Brutus and his men surrounded

---

42) LXI = *tan gwllt*, i.e. liquid fire. GoM has *suphureas tedas*, and *greco igne*. These are surprisingly early references to Greek Fire which, as Griscom points out (p. 537), was unknown to European writers until the Crusades of the Middle Ages - an added suggestion of the surprising antiquity of LXI's source material.
43) LXI = *Anakletys*.

the king's tent. Then Brutus blew his horn outside the tent, and they began to kill the Greeks as they slept.

And then the others awoke through the wails of the dying, not knowing where to flee until they [themselves] were slain [also]. And when the [Trojan] castellans had heard of it, they sallied forth [from the castle].

And when Brutus had entered the king's tent, he bound him fast, thinking that this would be more advantageous than killing him. And so, as morning dawned, Brutus summoned his men about him and divided amongst them the spoil of the slain, to each whatever he desired. And so Brutus came to the castle with the king as [his] prisoner, and he fortified the castle with men and weapons. And with the victory theirs, Brutus summoned his council to hear what he should demand of the king [for his ransom] - "For his life is in our hands, and he will give whatever we demand for his freedom."

And the council told him that it was better to receive from him a ransom than [to kill him and thus have to] live amongst enemies. And after a lengthy debate, a councillor named Membritius[44] arose, begged silence, and spoke after this manner: "O fellow councillors, for how long will you squabble in indecision over your best future interest, to wit to leave this place so that you and your children might live in permanent peace? For if you spare King Pandrasus, and demand of him a portion of Greece to live in, you shall never have real peace. So long as one Greek lives, they shall ever remember last night till they take vengeance for this battle either upon you or your children. Therefore I counsel you [Brutus] to take for your lawful wife she who is called Enogen,[45] his eldest daughter, and ships, with wine and provisions and all things necessary - and his agreement also, that we sail to wherever God may lead us as free men, lest the Greeks [once more] impose slavery upon us and our children!"

And they hailed his speech. And it was commanded that King Pandrasus be fetched before them, and Brutus declared that he, Pandrasus, would die if he did not consent to all their demands. And when he was brought before them, a seat was given him that was higher than all the rest. And he spoke after this manner: "The immortal gods have delivered both me and my brother, Antigonus, into your hands. And lest I forfeit my life, I am compelled to surrender to you, which I undertake to do in order to buy of you [both] myself and Antigonus, my brother. Nor is it shameful that I give to this young man my favourite daughter, for I know that he is descended of the lineage of Priam and Anchises,[46] as his

---

44) LXI = *Membyr.*
45) As in LXI. GoM has *Ignoge.*
46) LXI = *Enssisses.*

renown and heroism testify even now. Who but he could have freed the Trojan slaves after they had been held for so long under so many princes? Who else but he, with such a tiny army as his, could face the king of Greece, do him battle and defeat him, put his army to rout and finally capture him and hold him fast? To such as this I will give my daughter, and with her gold, silver, rare treasures, wine, oil, wheat, jewels, ships, and whatever else you might need. Or should you wish to remain here, I will bestow the third [part] of my realm [upon you], and remain a prisoner amongst you until you have obtained all [that I have] promised!"

And then messengers were despatched to every Greek port to collect ships and bring them to the one port, numbering in total three hundred and twenty-four vessels. And straightway they were laden with all the aforementioned goods, as well as all kinds of fruit. And then the king was released. And when they had all embarked, Enogen stood in the lowest part of the ship, weeping and crying for her homeland. And Brutus held her and spoke comfortingly to her, till, worn out with weeping, she fell asleep. And they sailed for two days and a night with a following wind until they landed on the island called Leucadia.[47]

And the island had been uninhabited and barren since having been devastated by pirates.[48] And Brutus sent ashore three hundred warriors to see if anyone lived there. And when they found no one, they hunted various animals. And as night fell upon them, they came across a vast and ancient ruined town. And there was a statue of Diana which spoke to whomsoever addressed it, and any who asked her a question, received an answer. And the next morning, they returned to their ships laden with game, and [they] told Brutus what they had discovered on the island. And they besought him to go to the temple and make sacrifice to the goddess, and ask of her which land he should dwell in.

And according to their counsel, Brutus took with him the wise man [named] Gerion[49] and twelve elders [of the people], and they, carrying with them

---

47) LXI = *legetta*. GoM = *Leogetia*, early Welsh and Latin forms respectively of Leucadia, an island of Thesprotia off the western coast of Greece. We know it today as Leucas or Levkas. The unexpectedly detailed geographical knowledge displayed by the original compiler of the source chronicle can hardly have been a guess on his part. Nor could it have been the work of some medieval forger, whose geography and available maps were, in any case, insufficiently capable of conveying such information. GoM, for example, tells in his Latin version of the island's woodlands, oak forests which are evident today on the island: "...the remnants of the oak forests which were a feature of Levkas well into the nineteenth century." (See Bradford, p. 48).

48) LXI = *Pirattas*. Assumed by the 12th-century translator to have been the name of a tribe, could this be an example of an early borrowing from the Latin (*pirata*) of post-Invasion times (1st century AD)? The Welsh for pirate has long been mor lleidr, lit. a sea-thief.

49) As in LXI. GoM has *Gero*.

everything they needed, went to the temple. And when he arrived there, Brutus placed on his head a laurel of vine leaves, and stood in the entrance of that ancient place of worship. And in accordance with ancient custom, sacrifice was made to the three gods, Jupiter,[50] Mercury,[51] and Diana.

And then Brutus stood alone before the altar of the goddess. In his left hand he held a vessel filled with wine. And in his right hand was a horn that was filled with the blood of a white hind. And he lifted his eyes to the image [of the goddess] and addressed her in this manner: "O thou who art the mighty Queen of the hunt, Protectress of the forest boar, O thou to whom it is given to ride the vault of Heaven and the halls of Hell, tell me which land I shall possess to dwell in, where I may worship thee through the ages and the years, and I shall build [in that place] a house in which to worship thee!"

And when he had repeated [these words] nine times, he walked four times around the altar. He then poured the wine between the lips of the goddess and lay down upon the pelt of a white hind.[52] And upon the third hour of the night, the time of deepest sleep, he dreamed that he saw the goddess before him, speaking in this manner: "Brutus," she said, "beneath the setting of the sun, beyond the land of Gaul, there lies an island in the sea in which giants once lived. It is empty now. Go there, for it is set aside for you and your descendants. And it shall be for your children like a second Troy, and kings shall be born of your line unto whom the whole earth shall pay homage!"

And after his dream, Brutus awoke, and wondered greatly at what he had dreamed. And they returned to the ships with joy, set sail, and, slicing through the waves of the sea, on the ninth day[53] they reached Africa.[54] And from there they knew not for which country they should steer. And they came to the Altars

---

50) LXI = *Iubiter.*
51) LXI = *Merkwri.*
52) The detailed knowledge of pagan ritual bears further testimony to the antiquity of the source material.
53) GoM gives thirty days for the voyage.
54) LXI = *Affric.* A strange fact emerges in the following itinerary which concerns the source material's seeming antiquity. The itinerary charts a course due west through the southern Mediterranean, naming points along the way that do not appear on any conventional map, either of the 12th century or today. These points would have been of interest only to a mariner navigating his way along and off this coastline. Moreover, its geography not only pre-dates the 8th-century Arab conquest of the North African countries, but pre-dates even the geographical reforms of that area conducted in the 1st century by Claudius Caesar. The names are all in the correct order for a westward voyage though no single ancient author lists all of them. Flinders Petrie supplies a detailed and telling discussion of the itinerary, providing Ptolemy's longitudes, and it would appear from this that the itinerary possesses an accuracy that is beyond any reasonable possibility of forgery or guesswork.

of the Philistines.[55]

And there they fell into great danger doing battle with cruel pirates.[56] But Brutus defeated them and increased his wealth with their spoil. From there they sailed to the land of Mauretania,[57] and through lack of food and water they must needs go ashore there and pillage the whole country. And from there they arrived at the Caves of the Mighty Hercules,[58] where they were surrounded by sea monsters who nearly sank their ships. And from there they came into the Tyrrhenian Sea,[59] and on the shore there met them four [other] groups of Trojan exiles who had escaped with Antenor. And a mighty man was prince over them who was called Corineus,[60] and he was stronger and braver than them all. And it was no harder for him to fight [against] a giant than [against] a boy of twelve months!

And when they had gained good intelligence of one another, and had learned that they all sprang from the same [Trojan] stock, they banded together, and Corineus paid fealty to Brutus. And through all [their] wars, he, Corineus, did more to strengthen Brutus['s hand] than any other. And they arrived [together] at Aquitania[61] and dropped anchor in the mouth of the Loire,[62] [remaining there] for seven days to get the lie of the land.

And the king of that land was Goffar the Pict,[63] and when he heard of the arrival of ships in his territory, he sent messengers to them to spy out their intentions, [whether it was] peace or war. And thus, as the messengers approached [where] the ships [lay], Corineus, who was hunting, intercepted them. And the messengers enquired of him with whose permission he hunted in the royal forest. And he answered that he needed no man's permission to hunt

---

55) LXI = *Velystinion.*

56) LXI = *piraniaid.* Again the translator of LXI takes this as the name of a tribe and not a translation of the Latin *piratae.*

57) LXI = *Mawretania.* LXI omits what GoM includes, namely the sailing of the fleet past the great salt lagoons, sailing between Russicada and the mountains of Zarec, and past the river Malve, all of which evidently was given in the original source material.

58) LXI = *erkwlff.* The Pillars of Hercules being the Strait of Gibraltar. Could the 12th-century translator have misread from a defaced original *ogof* (cave) for *colofn* (pillar)?

59) LXI = *mor tyren.* The Tyrrhenian Sea was an ancient name for the Atlantic Ocean.

60) LXI = *Koroneys.* Morgan (p. 27) informs us that he was also called *Troenius,* i.e. the Trojan.

61) LXI = *Ackwitania.*

62) LXI = *Lingyrys.*

63) LXI = *Koffarffichdi.* He was king of the Poitevins, a Pictish people. The modern city of Poitiers derives its name from them.

wheresoever he wished. With that, the messenger named Mynbert[64] drew his bow and loosed an arrow at Corineus, who evaded the arrow, straightway took hold of Mynbert, snatched the bow with great force from his hand, and hit him on the head with it, so that his brains adhered to the bow!

The other messenger hardly got away but by dint of speed, and he told Goffar the Pict how Mynbert had been killed. And then Goffar the Pict mustered a great army in order to wreak vengeance upon Corineus for slaying his messenger. And when Brutus heard this, he prepared his ships, placing the women and children [at a safe distance], and came ashore with his army [to fight] against Goffar the Pict. And they gave fierce battle [against him]. And Corineus was greatly ashamed that the Gascons[65] [so manfully] resisted them that the Trojans could not prevail. And Corineus summoned his [own] men and placed them on the right [flank] of the [enemy's] forces as a separate body. And he slew the enemy without respite, putting them to flight and leaving only the dead behind him. For when he wielded his two-edged axe, he slew whomsoever he encountered, slicing them from their heads down to the ground.

And his enemies were amazed as he did this, and he shouted these words after them: To where do you fly, you miserable cowards? [Stand and] do battle with Corineus! Away with you! Shame upon you {all] for fleeing from one man. But you do well to flee, for I would put even giants to flight!" As he said this, so Earl Suhard[66] turned back with a hundred warriors.[67] But Corineus attacked them, and, raising his axe, brought it down upon the crown of Earl Suhard's helmet and split him down to the ground.

And whirling his axe about his head, he slew his enemies without ceasing. And all who encountered him he slew or wounded with a single blow. And then Brutus, seeing him in danger, called his men to go to his rescue. And there was a mighty warfare between them and the several tribes [of Gascony], and Goffar the Pict was soon scattered with his army. And he went to his kindred in Gaul to seek allies [amongst them] in his rage against the men of Troy. And there prevailed at that time over Gaul but one usage as to dignity, lordship, and government, with twelve kings reigning. But King Karwed[68] ruled over them

---

64) As in LXI. GoM has *Himbert*.
65) LXI = *gwas gwniaid*. GoM (1:3) erroneously has the Aquitanians.
66) LXI = *ssiart*.
67) GoM has three hundred men at arms.
68) As in LXI. Curiously, GoM refers to this king though not by name. The Old Welsh *brenin karwed* can mean either a king named Karwed or the king of Karwed, so perhaps GoM could not decide which of the two was meant. I have elected here to translate Karwed as the king's name.

all. And these [kings] warmly welcomed Goffar amongst them, and promised to help him expel the foreign invaders from his country and its borders.

And when Brutus had gained the upper hand, he made his men wealthy with the spoils of the dead. And then, mustering his men to him a second time, he marched them to the interior and plundered the land of all manner of things, taking it all to the ships and burning the cities, taking all the gold and silver and anything else of value that they could carry, and slaying the people.

And then, after leaving all Gascony[69] in flames and ruins, he proceeded thence to the city of Tours.[70] There, finding a suitable place, he measured out a site for an encampment and raised a stockade about it, so that if necessary it might withstand an assault. For they, the Trojans, anticipated that Goffar the Pict would come with other kings and armies [against them]. And they awaited them there.

And once Goffar the Pict was aware that they were there, he marched [his armies] night and day until he arrived at a place where he might survey the entire encampment. And he cried, "Alas, alas! What fearful shame is this, to see a foreign people entrenched in my kingdom? Arm yourselves, my lords, and entrap them as sheep are trapped in the fold, and we shall divide them amongst ourselves and scatter them throughout the land as captives and slaves. And so shall we vent our anger and wreak our vengeance upon them!" And dividing his army into twelve divisions, he advanced upon the men of Troy.

When Brutus learned this, he donned his armour, [as did] his men also, and ferociously attacked Goffar the Pict, commanding his men to either attack or hold back as advantage required. And so, as the men of Troy vanquished the Picts, and caused Goffar the Pict to flee with his men at the first onslaught, two thousand[71] [of the Picts] were slain. But the numbers of Goffar the Pict's soldiers [combined with those of the men] of Gaul, were ten times those of Brutus. And each hour, more joined [the battle], and they attacked the men of Troy a second time, and having inflicted heavy casualties [amongst them], caused them to retreat again into their castles. And once the Gauls had won the day, they laid siege against the men of Troy, hoping to hem them in until either they died of starvation, or [until] they could devise some more cruel death [to inflict upon them].

And Brutus held counsel with Corineus that night, and it was decided that Corineus should steal quietly from the camp and conceal himself in a nearby

---

69) LXI = *gassgwin*. Again, GoM (1:14) has Aquitaine (see note 65).
70) LXI = *tyrri*.
71) GoM (1:15) calls Goffar's men Gauls.

wood, and that when Brutus should attack the Gauls the following day, he, Corineus, should arise and fall upon them [also], inflicting heavy losses on the Gauls. And Corineus did this, taking with him into the forest under cover of the night, three thousand warriors.

And in the morning, Brutus assigned his men their positions with great skill, and made battle against the Gauls in the field. And the Gauls retaliated ferociously, and many thousands fell on either side. And there was a young man of Trojan descent, a nephew of Brutus, whose name was Turnus.[72] And, second only to Corineus, he was the bravest [of the Trojans], for he had slain six hundred warriors with his own sword. But the Gauls finally killed him, and he was buried there in the place [where he died]. And that place still bears his name, and is called the city of Tours.[73]

And so Corineus fell upon the Gauls unawares, and attacked their rear without warning. And when Brutus knew of it, he braced himself and his men to courage, and so great was the noise that Corineus [and his men] raised, that the Gauls lost heart, believing that there was a mightier host in that place than there truly was. And the Gauls began leaving the field and fled, and the Trojans pursued them until they had vanquished them.

Now, although Brutus was glad of the victory, he was grieved by the death of Turnus his nephew, and the number of his men grew less by the day as the numbers of the Gauls increased. And because of this, Brutus was advised by his council to return to the ships whilst the victory was his and the greater part of his army was yet intact, and to make for the land of which the goddess had spoken. And straightway, through the counsel of his nobles, they boarded the ships and took with them whatever spoils they could find. And setting sail with a following wind, they came ashore on the beach at Totnes.[74] And the land was Albion, which in old Welsh[75] was called *Y Wen Ynys*.[76] And but for a few giants, it was uninhabited. Moreover, it was very fair to look upon, with fine rivers abundant with fish, and great forests also. And Brutus and his people were

---

72) LXI = *tyrri*.
73) Nennius (chap. 10) also relates this episode, calling the place *civitatem Turonorum*.
74) In Fore Street, Totnes, may still be seen the Brutus Stone on which Brutus is said to have stood when first he set foot on these shores (Westwood, p. 30). All of which may be more than mere tradition, for Manley-Pope (pp. 161-2) informs us of three Spanish historians who cite independently the migration of the colony to mainland Britain under Brutus, the writers being Florian de Campo (*Chronicle of Spain*, 1578), Estevan de Garabay (*Historical Compendium*, 1628), and Pedro de Roias (*History of Toledo*, 1654).
75) LXI = *kymraec*.
76) As in LXI. Britain doubtless gained the name of Albion or the White Island (*y wen ynys*) from the white cliffs of its south-eastern shore visible from Gaul.

delighted with the aspect of the island, and the giants sought refuge in the mountains.

And then, with leave of the princes, they divided the land amongst themselves, and they began to plough it and to build houses upon it and to settle it. And after only a short while, one would have thought that it had been settled for hundreds of years. And Brutus wished to call the land by his own name, and he decreed that the people dwelling therein should be called Britons,[77] also after his own name, for he craved a renown lasting to the end of time. And from that moment, the language of the people also was called British.[78]

And Corineus called that part [of the island] which fell to him, Cornwall,[79] for he was granted first choice before any other. And he chose that part of the land because therein dwelt the greatest number of giants, which he loved to fight more than any other thing. And amongst the giants of Cornwall there dwelt one who was mighty. He was called Gawr Madoc.[80] His height was twelve cubits, and his power and strength were so great that he could pluck from its roots beneath his feet the largest oak in the forest, as easily - or so it was said - as if he were plucking [from the ground] a sprig of hazel.

And behold, as Brutus, upon a feast day, was doing battle at that place where he first landed on this island, Gawr Madoc came with eleven [other] giants and inflicted great slaughter upon the Britons. But then the Britons rallied [together] and fought heroically against them, slaying every one of them except Gawr Madoc, for Brutus had ordained him to be saved alive because he wished to see Corineus fight him. And Corineus was overjoyed when he saw this great one approaching, and casting off his armour he challenged the giant to wrestle him. And they drew close to one another, face to face. And each took hold of the other amid such grunts and groans that they who watched nearby were troubled by their breath. And the giant straightway hugged Corineus with all his strength, breaking three of his ribs, two on the left side, and one on the right. And Corineus was filled with wrath. He summoned his might and lifted the giant to shoulder height, and ran with him to the highest point of the cliff's edge, throwing him over the cliff into the sea, dashing him into a thousand pieces.

And the waves were stained with his blood long after. And from that day to

---

77) LXI = *bryttaniaid.*
78) LXI = *bryttanec.* In all other references to the language, LXI uses *kymraec*, the language of the Kymry.
79) LXI = *kerniw.*
80) LXI = *gogmagoc.* GoM = *Gogmagog.* I have followed Manley-Pope here, who argues plausibly that *gogmagoc* may be nothing more than a later corruption of *Gawr Madoc*, Madoc the Great.

this, the place is called The Giant's Leap, or Gawr Madoc's Jump.[81] And when the land was at last divided, Brutus wished to build a city, and he travelled the length of the land looking for a suitable place for it. And he came finally to the banks of the Thames and walked along its sands. And when he found a most likeable place that met all his desires, he built there a city and named it New Troy.[82] And this was its name long after, until it became corrupted to Troinovantum.[83] In later times, it was ruled over by Lud,[84] the son of Heli, the brother of Cassivelaunus who did battle with Julius Caesar.[85] And when this Lud ruled the place, he fortified the city with great walls of wondrous workmanship, and enriched it with grants of land. And he ordered its name to be from then on, Caerlud,[86] after his own name. And the Saxons later called it London.[87] And for this reason there was great strife between Lud and Nennius[88] his brother, because the name of Troy was no more.

Now once Brutus had built the city, he girded it about with walls and towers, making them sacred and laying down immutable laws for the governance of such as should live there in peace. And he bestowed upon the city protection and privilege. And about this time was Eli the Priest ruler in Israel, and the Ark of the Covenant had been captured by the Philistines.[89] And in Troy there reigned a son of the mighty Hector once he had expelled from thence [the princes of] Antenor's line. And Silvius, the son of Ascanius, the son of Aeneas, ruled Italy, [being] the uncle of Brutus and the third ruler after Latinus.

And Brutus, by Enogen his wife, had three sons, Locrinus, Kamber and Albanactus. And when their father died in the four and twentieth year of his

---

81) Still known as Gogmagog's Jump, traditionally placed at Plymouth Hoe in Devon (Westwood, p. 30).
82) LXI = troyaf newydd, lit. New Troy. GoM (1:17) Latinizes the name to Troia Nova. One of the most ancient and persistent traditions amongst the Welsh up to modern times is that they are Lin Droea, of the lineage of Troy.
83) LXI = trynofant. GoM = Troia Nova and Trinovantum, extending this (rightly it seems) to the name of the Trinovantes who occupied Essex and Middlesex.
04) LXI – llydd.
85) LXI = ilkassar.
86) LXI = kaer lydd.
87) LXI = lwndwn, a phonetic rendering of its Saxon name. GoM traces the development of the name from Kaerlud, to Kaerlundein, to Londinium and hence to London.
88) LXI = rryniaw.
89) LXI = Pilistewission. The first of many synchronisms that help towards constructing a chronology for the early British kings.

reign,[90] they divided the land into three parts. Locrinus, the first-born, took the middle part of the island, which, from his name, was called Lloegria.[91] Kamber took that part beyond the Severn, which part was called Kymry.[92] And Albanactus received from the Humber up to Cape Bladdon that part [now] called Scotland, but from his name, Albany. And so all three ruled together.

And there came to Albany with a large fleet, Humber, king of the Huns.[93] And Albanactus fought with him there and was killed. And the people of that land were forced to flee to Locrinus. And he, Locrinus, summoned Kamber, his brother, and together they recruited the young men of both their kingdoms and met Humber in battle, putting him to flight. And he was drowned in that river that to this day bears his name, being called the river Humber.

And after the victory, Locrinus divided the spoils of the slain along with all the gold and silver found in the ships. And he took also three damsels who were lovely in face and figure, one of whom was daughter to the king of Germany,[94] whom Humber had taken captive with the other two damsels when he plundered the land. And her name was Estrildis,[95] and her skin was fairer than the whitest snow or the lily, or even walrus ivory. And when Locrinus beheld her, he was filled with love for her, and he took her to his bed as if she were his wedded wife.

But when Corineus heard of this, he was greatly angered because Locrinus was betrothed to his daughter. And so Corineus stood before the king, and waving his axe at him, spoke to him in this manner: "And is this how you repay me, sire, for the many wounds and injuries I endured when your father and I fought the barbarians together? And is this how you reward me, sire, by disgracing my daughter, preferring a heathen girl before her? You shall not do this thing cheaply while my arms have their strength, for by this axe have even

---

90) GoM has the twenty-third year. He further gives London as Brutus' burial place. Morgan (p. 31) narrows the place of burial down to *Bryn gwyn*, the White Mount, on which now stands the Tower of London. The White Tower may indeed derive its name from the earlier name.

91) LXI = *lloegr*, still the Welsh name for England.

92) Present-day Wales which, to native speakers, is still known as *Cymru*, (pr. *Goom-ree*).

93) LXI = *hymyr vrenin hvnawt*. This can mean either Hymyr, king of Hunawt, or Hymyr, a notable king. GoM (2:1) chooses the rendering *Rex Hunnorum*, king of the Huns.

94) LXI = *ssermania*, the land of the Germanic peoples. The Romans knew them as the *Allemani* (mod. Fr. *Allemagne*). Morgan (p. 33) follows this, giving the Welsh *Almaen*, which does not, however, appear in LXI. The term *ssermania* would thus appear to pre-date the Welsh adoption of *Almaen*.

95) LXI = *essyllt*. Transposed here as *Estrildis* (thus following GoM), Morgan (p. 33) tells us that she was also known as *Susa*.

giants met their deaths!"

And he made as if to strike the king with his double-edged axe, but their comrades rushed in betwixt him and the king. And having mollified them, they convinced Locrinus to take the daughter of Corineus for his wife. But for all that, he could not forswear his love for Estrildis, but provided for her in London[96] an underground chamber, and commanded his closest friends to guard her. And whenever he went to her, he pretended that he was going to sacrifice to God because, for fear of Corineus, he dared not take her openly to his bed.

But once Corineus was dead, Locrinus left Gwendolen,[97] the daughter of Corineus, and proclaimed Estrildis now to be his queen.

And Gwendolen, mourning, went to Cornwall and summoned all the young men of the province and declared war upon Locrinus. And the two armies met in battle on the banks of the river called Stour,[98] and a most furious battle was fought there. And there was Locrinus slain, being struck in the forehead by an arrow. And Gwendolen took into her own hands the rule of the land. And she commanded both Estrildis and her daughter, Habren, to be captured and drowned in the river which ever since has been called the Habren[99] throughout all Britain. And this shall be its name until the Day of Judgment because of the damsel who was drowned therein. And thus shall there be an everlasting memorial to the daughter of Locrinus.

And after Locrinus had ruled for twelve years,[100] the queen ruled twelve years more.[101] But when Maddan[102] her son came of legal age, he became king [of Lloegria], whilst she, Gwendolen, ruled Cornwall for the rest of her days. And Maddan wedded and of his wife had two sons, Mempricius and Malin.[103] And Maddan ruled the kingdom peacefully for twelve years,[104] and then he died.

---

96) LXI = *llyndain*. Morgan (p. 34) states that the chamber was built at *Caersws*, a city near the Severn.

97) LXI = *gwenddolav*.

98) LXI = *vyrram*, the river Stour in Dorset.

99) LXI = *hafren*. This tradition followed by Morgan (see note 96) is correct. The name of the river *Hafren* (still its Welsh name) was transposed by the invading Romans to *Sabrina*, hence the Severn.

100) GoM (2:6) states Locrinus reigned for ten years.

101) GoM (2:6) has fifteen years.

102) As in GoM (2:6). LXI = *madoc*.

103) As in GoM (2:6). LXI = *membyr* and *mael*.

104) GoM (2:6) gives Maddan's reign as forty years. Twelve years may be a scribal error where Gwendolen's twelve-year reign was accidentally attributed to Maddan.

Afterwards, a great quarrel arose between his two sons over the kingdom, for each wished to have it for himself. And Mempricius sent a message to his brother, Malin, to come and talk peace with him. But Mempricius treacherously caused his brother to be put to death, and after gaining the rule of the kingdom he became so wicked that he murdered as many noblemen as the island contained lest they should come to the throne after him. And he forsook his lawful wife, mother to the mighty Ebraucus, and gave himself up to the sins of Sodom and Gomorrah,[105] forsaking the natural use of his body. And in the hundredth year of his kingdom,[106] whilst hunting one day, he wandered away from his men in a wooded valley [where] wolves fell upon him and devoured him.[107]

And upon the death of Mempricius, Ebraucus[108] his son became king, and he ruled the kingdom stoutly for thirty years. And since the days of Brutus, he was the first to take ship to Gaul, which he ravaged and burned, pillaging gold and silver and returning victorious, having put whole cities to the flame, along with fortresses and castles. And he was the first to build in Albany, in the land beyond the Humber, the city named after him, Eboracum.[109] At about this time was David king in Jerusalem.[110] And he, Ebraucus, built the castle of Mount Angned, known today as Maiden's Castle or the Hill of Sadness.

And Ebraucus had twenty sons and thirty daughters by his twenty wives, and he reigned in the land for forty years. The eldest of his sons was Brutus Greenshield.[111] And then followed Sisillius, Regin, Morvid, Bladud, Lagon, Bodloan, Kincar, Spaden, Gaul, Dardan, Eldad, Ivor, Margodud, Cangu, Hector, Kerin, Rud, Asaracus, [and] Buel.

---

105) LXI = *ssotma* and *amorra*, two of the five cities of the Plain destroyed by God for their wickedness (Gen. 19).
106) GoM (2:6) has it in the twentieth year of his reign. Perhaps the Welsh chronicle means to convey that Membyr died one hundred years after Brutus founded the royal line. According to GoM's chronology, 108 years would have passed between that and Membyr's (Mempricius') death.
107) At this point, GoM inserts a double synchronism which is absent from LXI, namely that Saul ruled in Judea and Eurysthenes in Sparta at about this time (11th century BC).
108) LXI = *efroc*. According to GoM (2:7), Ebraucus ruled for thirty-nine years.
109) LXI = *dinas efroc*. GoM (2:7) employs the variant form *Kaerebrauc*. The city is known today as York, from the Viking *Yarvik*, which in turn is derived from the Roman *Eboracum*, thus perpetuating the name of its founder, Ebraucus.
110) LXI = *karissalem* (derived from *kaer salem*, city of peace?). This synchronism is added to by GoM, who says that Silvius was king in Italy at this time, and that Gad, Nathan and Asaph were prophets in Israel (11th -10th centuries BC).
111) GoM (2:8) adds the names of Ebraucus' thirty daughters.

And these sons and daughters were sent by their father to Italy, to Silvius Alba,[112] who was king after Silvius Latinus. And there they, the daughters, were wedded to the princes of the Trojan race. And all the sons, with Asaracus leading them, went to Germany with a fleet, and with help from Silvius Alba, they overran Germany and won the kingdom. But Brutus Greenshield remained [in Britain] with his father [to rule the kingdom after him], reigning for ten years.[113]

And the mighty Leil,[114] his son, came after. A good man was he, and a king who upheld truth and justice. And Leil ruled well over the government of the realm, and he built in the north of Britain the city of Carlisle.[115] And at this time did Solomon, son of David, build the Temple in Jerusalem. And there came the Queen of Sheba to hear the wisdom of Solomon.[116] And Leil ruled as king for twenty-five years. But in his latter days was he enfeebled, and civil war and disorder broke out in the realm.

And after him did Hudibras,[117] his son, reign forty years less one. And he delivered his people from war and brought them into peace, and built Canterbury and Winchester, and the town of Shaftesbury.[118] And in that place did the Eagle prophesy, foretelling doom to this land. And Solomon, the son of David, finished Jerusalem.

---

112) As in GoM. LXI = ssilmins Alban.
113) LXI = bryttys darian las. According to GoM, Brutus Greenshield reigned for twelve years. The epithet darian las (mod. Welsh tarian las) could equally mean Blueshield. I have followed GoM.
114) As in GoM (2:9). LXI = lleon.
115) As in GoM (2:9), who renders the name Kaerleil. LXI = kaer Lleon.
116) LXI = sselyf. GoM adds to this synchronism by stating that at this time Silvius Epitus succeeded his father, Silvius Alba, in the kingship of Rome.
117) LXI = Rvn baladr bras. GoM (2:9) transposes the name as Rud Hud Hudibras.
118) LXI = Kaer Kaint, and GoM = Kaer Reint for Canterbury. LXI = Kaer Wynt, and GoM has Kaerguenit for Winchester; and LXI = kaer Vynydd paladr (i.e. city of the Mount of Spears) for Shaftesbury.

And after Hudibras came Bladud,[119] his son, who ruled for twenty years. And he built Bath and the springs that were perpetually warm for any that had need of healing. And he worshipped the goddess Minerva. He learned the use of coals which burn to fine ash, but which flare up a second time into balls of fire. At about this time, the Prophets [in Israel] prayed that God would withhold the rain, and there was drought for three years and seven months.[120]

And Bladud was a deep and cunning man, the first in all Britain to talk with the dead. And he did not cease from doing such things until he had made for himself pinions and wings and flew high in the air, from where he fell to earth onto the Temple of Apollo in London, and was broken into a hundred pieces.

And after Bladud did Lear, his son, become king, and he ruled the kingdom with authority and in peace for forty years.[121] And he built a city on the river Soar called Caer Leir in the old Welsh, but in the Saxon tongue, Leicester.[122] And Lear, having no son, had three daughters, whose names were Goneril,

---

119) As in GoM (2:10). LXI = *blaiddyd*. GoM (2:10) agrees with LXI that Bladud reigned twenty years. He is said in other traditions to have discovered the 'virtues' of Bath's hot water springs by observing their effect on his pigs. Another tradition states that Bladud was a leper and the waters cured him. Interestingly, with these traditions in mind and especially that of his ill-fated attempt to fly, a Roman votive coin was found in the spring at Bath, an engraving of which appears in Camden's Britannica (see Manley Pope, p. 168). On the obverse is a winged head and the inscription *Vlatos* (Bladud), and on the reverse a unicorn with the legend *Atevla*, meaning a gift or vow. This dates the tradition to Roman times at the latest, when it is safe to assume that it was already very old. But of added force to the antiquity of the Bladud tradition is that on the island of Levkas (see note 47) on which Brutus landed with his followers in the first stage of their migration, there are the remains of a temple to the sun god Apollo (who in Greek mythology was the husband of Diana). These ruins lie on a prominence some 230 feet above the sea, and: "...it was from here that the priests of Apollo would hurl themselves into space, buoyed up - so it was said - by live birds and feathered wings. The relationship between the ritual and the god seems obscure, although there was an early connection between Apollo and various birds....Ovid confirms that the virtues of the flight and the healing waters below the cliff had been known since the time of Deucalion, the Greek Noah." (Bradford, p. 48). Bladud, it is recorded, also made himself pinions and wings and with them attempted to fly. But the intriguing detail is that he fell onto the temple of Apollo which stood in *Troinovantum*, present-day London.

120) See 1 Kings 17. This supplies an added synchronism.

121) LXI = *llvr*. GoM (2:11) = *Leir*. Much of this account has been immortalized in Shakespeare's King Lear. GoM tells us that Lear reigned for sixty years instead of LXI's forty. But this is the only discrepancy, which may indicate illegibility or damage to the source document.

122) LXI = *ssoram*, the river Soar. Leicester is rendered *kaer lvr* in LXI (Lear's city), but then LXI renders the name phonetically according to the Saxon pronunciation, *lessedr*.

Regan and Cordelia.[123] And their father loved them more than tongue can tell, loving Cordelia, his youngest daughter, above the other two.

And as he waxed old, weighed down with care, he thought to divide his realm into three parts, giving each part as a dowry for his daughters' husbands, a third of the realm with each [daughter]. And whichever of his daughters was discovered to love him most, to her would he give the largest portion of his wealth. And he asked his eldest how much she loved her father, and she protested that she loved her father more than the very soul in her body. And he said to her, "Because you love me more than all the world besides, my most loving daughter, I shall give you in marriage to that man whom most you love, and with you the third part of all my realm."

And next he asked his second eldest daughter how much did she love her father, and she replied that tongue could not tell how much she loved him, which was more than all creatures on earth. And Lear had great love towards her, and he granted her the second portion of all his realm.

And Cordelia, having seen her two sisters deceive him with a false and lying love, had thought to answer him with care. And so he asked his youngest daughter how much did she love her father. "My lord and father," [said she], "perchance there are those who make out that they love their father more than they truly do. But I, my lord, will love you as only a daughter should. I therefore love you as I should, but no more than this can I do, my lord and father."

So her father, suspecting that she said this out of malice of heart, was filled with anger, and said to her thus, "As you have loved me in my old age, so shall I love you from henceforth. I shall disinherit you forever of your share of Britain, and will bestow it upon your sisters. I do not say that I shall not give you to a husband, if the Fates so decree, for you are my daughter still. But I shall bestow upon you neither wealth nor honour as I have done to your sisters, for although I have preferred you always before them, me you have not loved!"

And so, by the counsel of his ministers, he betrothed his two elder daughters to two princes, to wit to the princes of Cornwall and of Albany,[124] and the two halves of the kingdom with them. But afterwards it came about that Aganippus,[125] king of Gaul, heard wonderful things of Cordelia, that she was

---

123) LXI = *Koronilla, rragaw*, and *kordalia*. I have given GoM's rendering (2:11).

124) As in GoM (2:11). LXI = *gogledd*. The *gogledd* was (and still is) the northern half of Britain, although its extent varies in our manuscript. Sometimes in LXI it is reckoned from the Humber to the whole of Scotland, and sometimes it coincides roughly with modern Scotland. Elsewhere in the manuscript the term *gogledd* seems merely to apply to North Wales. It is an indication of the different ages of the source material's component parts. A forger or fiction writer's use of the term would have been consistent.

125) As in GoM (2:11). LXI = *Aganipys*.

very beautiful. And he sent ambassadors to ask her father for her hand, and this [message] was conveyed to her father by them. And her father said that he would give her to him, but without a dowry in the world, for his wealth and his kingdom had been bestowed upon his other two daughters. And when the king of Gaul heard tell how fair the maiden was, he was filled with love for her, saying that he had gold, silver and lands enough and to spare. He had all things but a beautiful wife by whom he might beget heirs for his kingdom. And straightway they arrived at an agreement.

And then the two princes [of Cornwall and Albany] began to rule over the kingdom that he, Lear, had governed so stoutly and for so long, splitting it into two. And Maglaurus,[126] prince of Albany, took Lear into his care along with forty mounted knights with him,[127] lest he endure shame by lacking mounted retainers. And after Lear had lived with him for the quarter of a year,[128] Goneril took exception to the number of his retainers, for their [own] servants filled the court. So she complained to her husband that thirty were sufficient whilst the remainder should be dismissed. And on hearing of it, Lear said angrily that he would leave Maglaurus' household and go to the prince of Cornwall.

And the prince [of Cornwall] received him with honour. But at the end of the year, strife and conflict arose between the servants [of Lear and of the prince], and Regan lost patience with her father, ordering him to dismiss all his retainers save five only to serve him. And Lear became much distraught and left the court, and returned a second time to his eldest daughter, thinking that she would no longer begrudge that he kept his retainers with him. But she declared in great wrath that he should not stay with her unless he dismissed all his retainers save one who might wait upon him, saying that one as old as he had no need of such staff.

And when he perceived that his daughter would deny him all, he dismissed them all save one. And he bethought himself of his dignity and the honour [which he had lost], and thought of going to his daughter in Gaul. But he was afraid to do so, forasmuch as he had sent her there so lovelessly. But at the last, when he could no longer abide his other daughters, he left for Gaul, and once on board ship he saw that he possessed but three mounted knights to accompany him. And with weeping, he prayed in these words: "O Fates, where do you lead me? It is more grievous beyond measure to count wealth when it is lost than to

---

126) As in GoM (2:12). LXI = *maglawn*.
127) GoM (2:12) has one hundred and forty knights, suggesting damage or illegibility in the source document.
128) GoM has two months, again suggesting illegibility.

live even in poverty having never tasted riches. When I think of the hundreds who followed me as I warred against mine enemies, destroying castles and towns, and laying waste the land! But now I live in want and anguish at the hands of those who once were beneath my very feet. O God, when shall I have my revenge for this? Alas, Cordelia, how true were your words when you said that only as a daughter should love her father ought you to love me! When my hands were filled with riches, and it was given to me to bestow them, ah, how people loved me then! But where gifts are no more, then love has flown away.[129] How then shall I come to you and ask you to take me in, when I have given you so much offence? Of all their wisdom, yours was the greater, for once I had given them my realm, they cast me out of the land that was mine!"

And bemoaning thus his lot, he came to Paris,[130] the city where his daughter dwelt. And he sent to his daughter greeting, and told her what calamities had befallen him. And when his messenger told her that he, her father, was all alone save one servant who was with him, she sent him gold and silver, directing her father to go to a nearby city and obtain remedy there for his ills, bathe and dress himself in raiment fit for a king, and employ forty mounted retainers and fit them out sumptuously with horses, weapons and apparel. And he sent a message [of thanks] to his daughter and her husband. And when the king, Aganippus, heard what was happening, he came with his nobility to greet him, and welcomed him as a king - with honour.

And Aganippus gathered together a mighty host from amongst the Gauls, even mounted knights. And they came to Lloegria, Lear and his daughter Cordelia and all the host with them, for to do battle with his two sons-in-law. And they defeated them every one. And after Lear regained his kingdom the second time, he lived for but three years. And at that time came Aganippus, king of Gaul, and Cordelia obtained the realm in her own right. And she buried her father in an underground chamber which was built beneath the river Soar at Leicester. And his tomb was dedicated to the god Janus.[131] And [in honour of this god], there gathered together at the beginning of the year all the cunning workmen and artificers of the realm to begin each project that they planned to

---

129) And interesting and rare preservation of an ancient Celtic proverb.
130) Founded by an early Celtic people called the *Parisi*, some of whom settled later in present-day Yorkshire. GoM (2:12), however, names the city as *Karitia*, by which some scholars think that Calais is meant. But it may simply be another example of illegibility giving an uncertain reading, having only the letters common to *Kariti* and *Parisi* discernable in the original source document. I have followed LXI in assuming that the reading Paris is intended.
131) As in GoM (2:14). LXI = *biffrons*.

complete by the end of that year. And Cordelia ruled her people in peace and great joy.[132]

And afterwards her two nephews rebelled against her, being her sisters' sons, the son of Maglaurus, prince of Albany, and the son of Henwinus, prince of Cornwall. And these sons were named Marganus,[133] the son of Maglaurus, and Cunedagius,[134] the son of Henwinus. And they proclaimed it a sorrowful thing for a woman to rule the land. And so each of them warred against her and laid waste the kingdom. And they fought with her and cast her into prison where, out of anger and despair, she took her own life.[135]

And these men shared between them the two halves of the kingdom, to Marganus the part beyond the Humber called Scotland, and to Cunedagius fell all the rest. And after two full years of this, there came to Marganus certain men who loved strife, telling him that it was scandalous for him to rule only the half when, being the elder, he ought to rule the entire kingdom, and that Cunedagius possessed the greater part. And Marganus began laying waste the land. But Cunedagius mustered a great army against him and put him to flight, pursuing him from place to place until they came, at last, to a great plain in Wales. And a battle ensued in which Marganus was slain near the place where stands the abbey of Margam, in which he lies buried.

And having gained the victory, Cunedagius ruled the entire kingdom for thirty-three years in contentment and peace. And about this time, on the eleventh day before [the feast of] Beltain, Rome was begun by the brothers Romulus and Remus.[136] And once Cunedagius was dead, Rivallo,[137] his son, ruled after him. And he was a comely young man who brought peace and great joy [to the land]. He governed his people in tranquillity, and in his time there fell a rain of blood for three days and nights, and men perished.

And after Rivallo, Gurgustius,[138] his son, was anointed king. And after him ruled Sisillius.[139]

---

132) GoM gives five years for her reign.
133) As in GoM (2:15). LXI = *morgan*.
134) As in GoM (2:15). LXI = *kynedda*.
135) lit. 'she lost herself'.
136) A further synchronism dating these events with the foundation of Rome, i.e. ca. 753 BC. GoM (2:15) adds the ministry of the prophet Isaiah to this.
137) As in GoM (2:16). LXI = *rriallon*.
138) As in GoM (2:16). LXI = *gorwst*.
139) As in GoM (2:16). LXI = *Saissyll*.

And after him, Iago,[140] the nephew of Gurgustius, took the crown. And after Iago, Kimarcus,[141] the son of Sisillius, was king. And after him did Gorboduc[142] rule. And Gorboduc had two sons, called Ferrex and Porrex.[143]

And when their father became weakened by age and disease, a deadly quarrel arose between the two brothers concerning the crown and who should inherit it. Porrex, moved with anger and contempt for his brother, conspired in his heart to murder him. And when Ferrex learned of it, he fled to Gaul to seek aid and succour from Suhard,[144] the Gaulish king. And he returned to do battle with his brother, and Ferrex slew him with the greater part of his army.[145] But their mother[146] was wroth with Ferrex, her surviving son, and crept in with her maidservants and found him asleep. Whereupon she slew him whilst he slept, and ripped his flesh from his body.

And for a long time after, there was civil war[147] and strife throughout the realm. And the kingdom was rent into five parts, each part under its own king, which kings continually fought one another. And after many years there arose a famous youth named Dunvallo Molmutius.[148] He was the son of Cloten,[149] a petty king of Cornwall, and his beauty and courage outshone that of all the kings of Britain. And this same young man, when his father died, took over the

---

141) As in GoM (2:16). LXI = *Kynvarch*.
142) As in GoM (2:16). LXI = *gwrvyw*.
143) As in GoM (2:16). LXI = *ffervex* and *porex*.
144) As In GoM (2:16). LXI = *Siwart*.
145) Apparently a copyist's error for *Porrex*. LXI has, confusingly, *fforex*. This is of some interest, for it was to cause confusion for subsequent historians. Fabyan, the Tudor chronicler, complains that "...here discordyth myn Auctour with some other wryters and with the Chronycle of England, for they testyfye that Porex was slayne & Ferrex survived...."
146) Unnamed in LXI, GoM (2:16) names her as *Judon*. Fabyan calls her *Widen*, and Manley Pope (pp. 169-70) adds: "According to the authorities:- When the partizans of her son, who were near at hand, had heard and seen that this terrible deed" [i.e. the murder of Porrex] "was done, they took her and put her in a sack, and threw her alive into the Dain (Thames), where she was drowned. The two sons thus having died without issue...with them...ended the direct line of Brutus." Manley Pope cites his source for this as: Welsh MS. Chro. (Jones).
147) According to the chronology of the Welsh chronicle (and GoM), this civil war lasted about two hundred years. Its cause, of course, was the extinction of Brutus' line. After this period the British crown was as much a matter of election as heredity.
148) As in GoM (2:17). LXI = *Dyfnal moel myd*. The Molmutine Laws have in fact survived.
149) As in GoM (2:17). LXI = *klydno*.

governance of the realm, and he straightway slew Pinner,[150] king of Lloegria.

And when Rudaucus,[151] king of Kymry [or Wales], heard of it, and Staterius,[152] king of Albany, they brought their armies into Dunvallo's land and began to pillage it and burn it. And Dunvallo, on hearing this, came against them with an army of thirty thousand, and did battle with them, and most of the day was spent with neither side gaining the upper hand.

And Dunvallo summoned to him one hundred and twenty of his bravest warriors,[153] and he divided amongst them the armour [of the enemy slain]. And throwing off his own armour, he also put on the armour of a slain enemy, and marching quickly to the place where Rudaucus was, he slew him. And with his hundred and twenty warriors, he ran to the place where also was Staterius, and he killed him also. And he accomplished all this with but a hundred and twenty men. And donning again his own armour, lest his own men should slay him, he exhorted his soldiers once again to slay their enemies. And presently he won the field, afterwards crossing the land from coast to coast, burning castles and encampments as he went.

And when he had rendered all Britain subservient to himself, he commanded a crown of gold to be made for him, and he wore it upon his head. And he restored the land to its ancient dignity, and compiled laws which are known [to this day] as the laws of Dunvallo Molmutius, which even the Saxons obey. And he granted right [of sanctuary] to temples and to cities, and even to certain roads defined by law, so that any man who fled to them, whatever wrong he had done, should find sanctuary there unimpeded and without licence from his foes.

And Gildas tells of other things that were done by this king, too numerous to mention, for he also gave right of sanctuary to the principal highways leading to all the chief cities. And these same roads he granted to the common people [so] that they might go to the cities [unmolested], for in his day was tolerated neither thief nor footpad.[154] And having governed the realm in this manner forty years from the time that he first wore the crown, he died, and was buried in

---

150) As in GoM (2:17). LXI = *pymed*. It may be that this was not the personal name of this king, as *pymed* means 'fifth' in Old Welsh, and reference has just been made in the text to the five petty kingdoms caught up in the civil war. "The fifth king" might be a more accurate rendering.
151) As in GoM (2:17). LXI = *nydawc*.
152) As in GoM (2:17). LXI = *tewdwr*, the earliest appearance of the name Tudor.
153) GoM (2:17) has six hundred warriors.
154) Flinders Petrie and Probert (see Bibliography) discuss the entirely pagan nature of Dyfnal's laws, which dates them to well before the coming to Britain of Christianity.

London in a famous temple of his own building.[155] .

And following his death, quarrelling and discord broke out between his sons Belinus[156] and Brennus[157] over the realm and who should govern it, for each of them desired the crown for himself. But learned men of great wisdom made peace between them, and they divided the realm into two parts. And because Belinus was the eldest son, he obtained Lloegria and Kymry, with Cornwall besides. This was in accordance with the ancient laws of Troy concerning the firstborn's inheritance. And to Brennus fell the whole of the country north of the Humber, all of Albany, but in subjection to his brother. And this was agreed between them and five years of peace went by.

Then those who hated peace, came to Brennus, telling him that it was timid and disgraceful of him to yield his rights to his brother, they both being born of the same parentage and holding the same rank. Moreover they said, "You are more wise in battle than he, for when Cheulfus, the prince of the Moriani,[158] came into your realm, you straightway chased him out of it. Break this humiliating agreement, therefore, that stands between you and your brother, and go to the king of Lochland[159] and take his daughter for your wife. And then, with him as ally, you shall win back your right!"

And Brennus was spurred on to great anger by their counsel, and he went to Lochland and wedded the daughter of its king. And when Belinus heard of this, he was wounded in heart and bethought it great treachery that his brother had sought this alliance against him. And Belinus mustered a mighty army and marched across the Humber and captured castles and towns, manning them with his own soldiers.

And hearing of this, Brennus summoned a mighty host from Lochland. And [when he was] sailing cheerfully with his fleet towards his own land, behold,

---

155) GoM (2:17) specifies that this was the Temple of Concord. Did this stand of the present site of St Paul's?

156) As in GoM (3:1). LXI = *beli*.

157) As in GoM (3:1). LXI = *bran*.

158) As in GoM (3:1). LXI = *Edwetro*, who is prince (*tywysog*) of the *Morien*.

159) GoM (3:1) supplies the name *Elsingius* for the king in question. LXI simply calls him *brenin Ilychlyn*, the king of Lochland. The country of *Ilychlyn* which translates as Lochland, or Land of the Lochs, is said by GoM to be Norway. Rhys, however, in his Celtic Heathendom (p. 355), correctly identifies *Ilychlyn* with the western coast of present-day Scotland. GoM's confusion seems to have arisen through the Norwegians' one-time claim that this part of Scotland properly belonged to Viking Norway,and the medieval (and earlier) mind would naturally have equated the claimed territory with Norway itself. But wouldn't you know it, just to confuse matters further, *Llychlyn* is known in modern Welsh as Scandinavia in general.

Guthlac,[160] king of the Danes, for love of the woman to whom Brennus was now wed, pursued him. And when he, Guthlac, had sighted the ship wherein Brennus was sailing, he did battle against him until with grappling irons he captured his ship, in which also was Brennus' wife, and towed it back into the midst of his own fleet. Whereupon, of a sudden there came a mighty, calamitous wind which scattered the ships to every shore, and in this way they sailed for five days. And the king of the Danes came ashore on the coast of Albany, and on hearing of it the men of that land captured them and brought them before Belinus, who was awaiting his brother from Lochland.

And besides the vessels of the Danish king, there were three others also belonging to Brennus. And Belinus seized them with joy and began to avenge himself against his brother. And Brennus arrived after some days, having gathered his fleet together from along the coast of Albany. And he heard tell that Belinus had seized both his men and his wife. And he sent to his brother commanding him that he restore his wife and his kingdom to him again, and he would slay him also if he met him. And when Belinus heard it, he scorned the demands, both concerning his wife and his realm. And then Belinus mustered together an army of all the mounted warriors of Britain, and prepared to meet Brennus in battle.

And no sooner had Brennus learned of this, than he came against Belinus at a place called the Forest of Caledonia,[161] and there did they bravely fight one another, for their renown in battle was great. And men fell on either side like ears of corn before the reapers. And at last the Britons won the day, sending the army of Lochland a broken [army] back to its ships. And in that battle there fell fifteen thousand men of Lochland, and not one escaped unharmed. And Brennus did scarcely reach one of the ships, and he fled to Gaul. The remainder sought refuge wherever they might find it.

And now, having vanquished his foes, Belinus called together all the nobility of the realm to Eboracum, that he might seek counsel concerning the king of the Danes. For he, Guthlac, had sent ambassadors to him, offering homage and fealty and annual tribute so that he and his loved one might be granted their freedom. And Belinus allowed [his petition] according to counsel, and required at his hand vows [of fealty] from the king of the Danes, and hostages also. Then he, Guthlac, and she whom he loved, were set free. And

---

160) LXI = *Gwychlan*. GoM (3:2) = *Ginchtalacus*.
161) LXI = *Kaladyr*. GoM (3:3) names the forest as that of *Calaterium*. Thorpe (p. 311) thinks that this term applies to the wilds of Scotland, noting in passing that another identifies it as Celidon Wood near Lincoln. Given that Albany is the background of events here, then a wood in Scotland seems the most likely location.

when Belinus had pacified the kingdom from end to end, there was none to withstand him. And he confirmed the laws and proclaimed peace throughout the land as well in the temples as in the cities, which he blessed with unheard of privileges.

And in those days there arose disputes concerning the highways, whose borders were not clearly defined. And so he, Belinus, summoned before him all the stonemasons of Britain, and commanded them to build roads of stone and mortar, according to law. And one of the roads ran through such cities as lay in its path from the tip of Cornwall up to Cape Bladdon[162] in Albany, the entire length of Britain. And another was built at his command to run across the land from Menevia[163] on the one coast to Port Hamon on the other, the same being Southampton.[164] And two other roads also he caused to be laid, running obliquely from corner to corner, passing, as did the others, through the cities [that lay in their path]. And when all was done, he commanded that they be held sacred, and bestowed upon them the right of sanctuary [so] that none dare molest whoever sought refuge there, however grievous his offences might be. And after these things did Belinus rule in peace.

And Brennus, his brother, who had sought refuge in Gaul, was grieved for his exile from his land and his realm. And he could not regain it, and knew not what he should do. And so, with eleven servants,[165] he stood before the king of Gaul and laid before him all his woes. And when he, the king of Gaul, disdained to help him, he went straightway to the king of Burgundy,[166] who welcomed him warmly and granted him audience, and bestowed honour upon him above all his court. For in all that he did, Brennus acted with honour, and the king loved him just as if he were his son. For Brennus was handsome and courtly to look on, and was learned and able, as a prince ought to be.

And after the king had bestowed his love upon him, he gave to Brennus for his wife his only daughter and heir, and bequeathed Burgundy to him when he should succeed him, provided the king should have none other heir. But if he, the king, should yet have a son, then he would strengthen the hand of Brennus that he might win back his own realm. And one of the princes also promised him help. And so Brennus wedded the girl, and the nobility of the land became

---

162) GoM (3:5) = *Caithness*.
163) LXI = *kaer vyniw*, present-day St David's.
164) Part of this road lays beneath the modern A36 out of Southampton.
165) GoM (3:6) has twelve knights.
166) As in GoM (3:6), who also identifies him as *Segnius*, lord of the Allobroges or Burgundians. Segnius appears as *Segovesus* in Livy (p. 379). In LXI, Burgundy appears as *byrgwin*.

subject to him, and he governed the land that was granted him of the king with his own hand. And Brennus restored to these nobles who were loyal the lands which the king had taken from their fathers, and in this manner did he bind their loyalty and love through his own kindness. And his hospitality was renowned throughout all the realm, for he fed and watered all who came to him, closing his doors upon no man.

And once he was certain that the hearts of all his people were with him, he bethought himself how he might avenge his hurt upon Belinus his brother for the things that he had done to him. And all his subjects swore loyalty to him and promised him arms for to subdue any place in all the earth that he might wish to conquer. And straightway he gathered a mighty host, and coming to Gaul he sought their permission to pass through their land unmolested toward Britain. And when the fleet was made ready upon the Flanders coast, they sailed with a following wind till they landed in Britain.

And once Belinus knew that his brother was coming with a navy, he mustered a mighty army and sallied forth to meet him, that they might do battle together. And then, as they were about to close in on each other, so Tonwen, their mother, did run through the host and came to them, pleading to see Brennus her son, for she had not set eyes upon him for many a year. And, shaking with fear, she went to the place where her son Brennus was standing, and kissed him many times. And then she made naked her breasts, and weeping bitterly spoke these words to him: "My beloved son, remember these breasts upon which you have sucked, and remember your mother's love for you who carried you nine months in her womb. And remember all that I suffered to raise you [to manhood]. Think on these things this day, and for the sake of your heavenly Creator, forgive your brother. Let that wrath be still which you have nurtured against him, for he gave you no reason to hate him so. It was not he who banished you from your land and your realm, for he has done you no harm. And in all that he did, he did nothing to humiliate you. But rather he has raised you up, for though you once were in subjection to him for the lesser part of the realm, you are now his equal in dignity. Surely, it is a far greater honour to be prince of all Burgundy, than to rule only a small part of Britain. And recall that this quarrel between you was not caused first by him, but by you when you sought the hand of the daughter of Lochland's king, and through that alliance sought to bring down your brother!"

And when she had spoken these words with much weeping, he resolved in his heart to follow all his mother's bidding and live in peacefulness and quiet. And taking his helmet and cap of mail from off his head, he approached to where his brother was standing. And when he, Belinus, saw his brother draw nigh, he cast aside his weapons and embraced him. And so were they soon reconciled. And their hosts, welcoming the peace, also cast down their weapons. And they, Belinus and Brennus, marched to London where they held council, both they and the nobility. And they determined to go to Gaul and take possession of it, and all its provinces.

And having stayed in London for a year, they marched out towards Gaul, and began to lay the land waste. And hearing of it, the men of Gaul rallied together into one place to withstand them, but Belinus and Brennus vanquished them every one. And the men of Gaul fled the field, but the Britons pursued them till they captured their king and forced him to yield. And the Britons demolished the castles and subdued the whole realm within the year. And after, they descended with their hosts onto the land of Rome, where they destroyed castles throughout all Italy and laid waste the land as far as Rome [itself].

Now in those days two consuls governed Rome, Galens and Porsenna,[167] to whom was entrusted the government of the land. And when they perceived that none could resist the might of Belinus and Brennus, by the counsel of the Senate of Rome they sought to establish peace with them, offering them a great tribute of silver and gold, promising the same for every year should they leave them in peace. And for token of the pledge, Belinus and Brennus took hostages of them.

And Belinus and Brennus took their armies from that place, and set out for Germany. But once they became embroiled in conflict with these tribes, they, the Romans, repented of the promise that they had made to the Britons, broke their word, and went to the aid of the Germans. And Belinus and Brennus were enraged to hear of it, and they bethought themselves how they might vanquish two armies at once, for the coming of the Roman army was a great threat. And they decided to leave Belinus with the Britons to overcome the Germans, whilst Brennus and his [Burgundian] host sought to overrun Rome.

---

167) As in GoM (3:9). LXI = Galins and fforkena. Porsena, though not actually given in Livy's account of the Gaulish Invasion of 390 BC, is known to be a very ancient Roman name and not one that would normally be expected to appear in Old Welsh. GoM's Gabius (identified by LXI as Galins) seems to be a garbled memory of one Quintus Fabius whom Livy most surely mentions. Quintus Fabius (Livy, pp. 3812) heroically charged the Gaulish lines, which provoked the subsequent sacking of Rome. The Gaulish army knew him to have come from Rome, and it is therefore natural that they should have supposed him to be acting on Rome's behalf. There is further confusion of detail between LXI and Livy, but this only demonstrates that LXI is no mere rehash of Livy, whose history of Rome was in any case not available in 12th-century England. The Beli of the Welsh chronicle is Bellovesus in Livy, the nephew of Ambitgatus, king of the Bituriges. The Bituriges were the Celtic tribe inhabiting the west central region of France, who gave their name to the city of Bourges. Beli's mother (unnamed in LXI) is called Tonuuenna in GoM, and she was clearly the sister of Ambitgatus, marriages between the royal families of the British and Continental Celts being the common practice. Bran in LXI is Brennus in Livy, the leader of the Gaulish Invasion, and it is interesting to compare the two accounts of the invasion as seen through the eyes of Livy and the Welsh chronicler. It seriously challenges those theories that have lately attempted to dismiss Beli and Bran as mere personifications of Celtic gods.

And learning of this, the Roman army abandoned the men of Germany and tried to overtake Brennus and his army before they reached Rome. And when Belinus heard of it, he brought his army against them by night into a wooded valley that lay in their path. And Belinus concealed himself and his men there to ambush them. And behold, arriving in that place the following day, and seeing the weapons of their foes gleaming along the valley, the men of Rome feared greatly, thinking that Brennus and the Burgundians were there. And Belinus suddenly fell upon them, and the Romans straightway fled the field, being unable either to don their armour or make a stand. And Belinus pursued them until darkness prevented further slaughter.

And after vanquishing his foes, Belinus reached Brennus his brother on the third day after he, Brennus, had dug in around the walls of Rome. And when the two armies were come together before the city, they laid siege to it and assaulted it mightily, bringing great suffering upon the people of Rome. And they built a scaffold before the city gates, upon which to hang the hostages should they, the people of Rome, not surrender the city. But the Romans held the city nonetheless, and they resisted now with catapults and at other times with ballista, using whatever means [of resistance] they could find. And when Belinus and Brennus saw it, they burned with indignation, and ordered the hanging of twenty-four hostages of the highest rank before the city gates.

And then the men of Rome marshalled their troops into divisions and poured out of the city and engaged them in open battle, for word had reached them from the two captains who had regrouped their scattered troops, that they were marching to their rescue, and they were on no account to surrender the city. And the [Roman] army fell suddenly upon the Britons in two divisions, and there was great bloodshed.

And when Belinus and Brennus beheld their troops being slaughtered, it grieved them and they rallied their soldiers, exhorting them to resist the foe. And they withstood them, and, at last, when thousands on either side had fallen, Belinus and Brennus overcame the men of Rome. [And they] slew Galens[168] and captured [both] Porsenna and the city.

And Belinus and Brennus divided the spoil amongst their army. And having won the day, Brennus ruled Rome as a tyrant,[169] and he governed the people with great cruelty. But as all this is rehearsed in the histories of the Romans, I have here not told the half of it for the weariness of telling all.

---

168) Livy doesn't mention the death of Quintus Fabius, which again contradicts any notion of copying.
169) As elsewhere in LXI, the term 'emperor' (*ymerawdwr*) is used here with typical Celtic looseness. Tyrant might convey the meaning better.

And Belinus returned to Britain and governed the realm in peace for the rest of his days. And he repaired the castles, whichever of them lay in ruins, and built new ones also. And beside these things, he built a city on the banks of the Usk, and established there the arch-druidship of Dyfed.[170] And when the Romans came [later] to these shores, they called it the City of Legions, for they kept their winter-quarters in that place. And Belinus caused to be built a marvellous gate in London on the banks of the Thames, which was called Belin's Gate.[171] And upon its battlements he constructed a great tower, and at its foot a wharf for the mooring of ships. And everywhere he ratified his father's laws and upheld truth. And there was great wealth among the people in his days, the like of which was not seen before or after. And at last, when the day of his death was come, his body was cremated and his ashes sealed in a golden urn of wondrous craftsmanship, which was buried within the top of that tower in London, of which we have already spoken.

And at the death of Belinus, his son, Gurgant the Peaceful,[172] took up the crown. And he was an honest man, following in his father's ways of loving peace and truth. But if any should come against him, he put on a soldier's courage, and fought and vanquished his enemies, making them his subjects. And the king of the Danes tried to withhold the tribute that he had paid to his father. And he, Gurgant, took ship against the king of the Danes and warred mightily against him. And he killed the king and placed the country in subjection to himself, [even] as it was formerly in subjection to his father.

And as he was returning home past the Orkney Isles, he encountered thirty ships full of men and women. And he seized their leader, named Partholan,[173] who begged his protection, claiming to have been exiled from Spain and having sailed the ocean in his search for a land to live in. And he besought Gurgant for a portion of this island to dwell in, that they might no more be tossed upon the seas, for they had been at sea for one year and a half.

And when Gurgant had learned of them their nation,[174] he had them taken to the land of Ireland, which was then uninhabited, and bestowed that land upon

---

170) As in LXI. GoM (3:10) = *Demetia*.
171) As in GoM (3:10). LXI = *Bilinssgad*, seemingly a phonetic rendering of the Saxon name.
172) LXI = *Gwrgant varf drwch*. GoM (3:11) = *Gurguit barbtruc*, a clumsy Latin rendering of the Welsh. I have translated the name as Gurgant the Peaceful, preferring this to the alternative, Gurgant Grim-Beard (the meaning of GoM's Latin), *drwch* being related, I feel, to the modern Welsh *trugarog*, meaning Merciful or Compassionate.
173) LXI = *Bartholome*. GoM (3:12) = *Partholoim*. According to the Irish Chronicles, Partholan founded the Irish monarchy in ca 15th century BC, which causes a discrepancy of more than a thousand years between the British and Irish chronologies.
174) GoM (3:12) adds the information that they were *Basclenses*, or Basques.

them in perpetuity. And the people multiplied and settled the land, and their descendants are in Ireland to this day.[175] And when Gurgant reached the end of his days, he died in Caerleon-on-Usk, and there was he buried in a place that he had fortified after his father's death.

And after Gurgant's death, Guithelin,[176] his son, ruled the realm, and he governed it peacefully and quietly until the end of his days. And his wife was named Marcia, and she was learned in all the arts, having discovered with her husband all manner of things concerning the foundations of the laws. And these [laws] the Britons called the Laws of Marcia,[177] which laws did Alfred the king translate from Old Welsh into Saxon, and called it the Mercian Code[178] in the Saxon tongue.

And when Guithelin died, his wife ruled both in his stead and in that of his son, for Sisillius[179] was barely seven years of age at his father's death, and was disqualified from the crown because of his years. But his mother wisely kept him at her side, so that when she died Sisillius took up the crown.

And after him, Kinarius,[180] his son, was made king. And after him, Danius,[181] his brother, took the crown. And after him, his son Morvid[182] did rule, who was his son through a concubine.[183] And he [could have] earned every man's praise but for his love of cruelty, for in wrath he forgave no man, but would slay him if he might. Yet was he handsome and generous, and in battle there was not his like in all the realm. And in his days came Morien[184] with a great army into Albany, and he laid waste the land. And Morvid came against him with his host, and Morvid killed more of the foe single-handedly than did any of his warriors. And having won the day, he left not a man of the enemy alive, but commanded that they all be brought before him, each in his turn, to

---

175) LXI = *Iwerddon*. Cusack tells us: "This account was so firmly believed in England, that it is specially set forth in an Irish act (11th of Queen Elizabeth) among the 'ancient and sundry strong and authentique tytles for the kings of England to this land of Ireland'."
176) As in GoM (3:13). LXI = *Kyhylyn*.
177) LXI = *Marssia*. GoM (3:13) = *Lex Martiana*.
178) LXI = *Maicheneange*.
179) LXI = *Saessyllt*, the second to own this name.
180) As in GoM (3:14). LXI = *kynvarch*.
181) As in GoM (3:14). LXI = *daned*.
182) LXI = *Morydd*. GoM (3:14) = *Morvidus*.
183) GoM (3:14) tells us that she was named *Tanguesteaia*.
184) More properly not the name of an individual, but a people, the Moriani. Known to Julius Caesar as the *Morini*, they were a people who previously had troubled Beli and Bran. They occupied the French and Belgian coasts between modern-day Zeebrugge and Boulogne.

be skinned alive and then killed. And having rested for a while, he commanded the others to be skinned and then burned alive.

But there arose a terror to undo his sin and wickedness, for from the direction of the Irish Sea there came a dragon,[185] whose hunger could never be satisfied. Wherever he might be, he devoured both man and beast without ceasing. And when Morvid learned of it, he went there himself to kill it. But it availed him nothing, for he had run out of all his weapons when the dragon fell upon him and devoured him alive, gulping down his body as a great fish gulps down a little one.

And this man had three sons, one of whom, [the eldest], was named Gorvonion[186] the Just. And he ascended the throne as a righteous king, for none loved justice more. And in all the cities of Britain, he repaired the places of worship and built new ones, for in those days was there an abundance of gold and silver. And he caused the people to till the land, and he protected them from any wrong at the hand of noble or prince. And he ensured that the young men had ample wealth, so that none of them need wrong another. And Gorvonion passed away and was buried in London.

And after him, Arthal,[187] his brother, was king. But he was not like his brother in his rule, for he dispossessed the hereditary nobility and raised the unworthy to office, robbing the wealthy and the good, and compelling them to pay him taxes. And at last, the nobility of the realm rebelled against him and deposed him. And they made Elidyr[188] the Good king in his place, calling him the Good for the mercy he showed to his brother. For when five years were ended, Elidyr was out hunting in the Caledonian Forest, when, as chance would have it, he met Arthal his brother who had been banished the realm. And he had been to many lands seeking help to recover his crown, but all to no avail. And being unable any longer to endure such dreadful want, he had come back again into Britain with but twelve mounted knights, hoping to see again his half-brothers. And when Elidyr saw him, he rushed to embrace him and threw his arms about him and kissed him. And Elidyr wept for him, for his exile, and for his terrible misfortunes.

And then Elidyr went with his brother to the town of Alclud,[189] and concealed him there in a secret place. And Elidyr gave out that he, Elidyr, was

---

185) GoM (3:15) calls the creature a *Belua*, a generic Latin term for any monstrous beast.
186) LXI = *Gwrviniaw*. GoM (3:16) = *Gorbonianus*. He was the first king to bear this name.
187) As in LXI. GoM (3:17) = *Archgallo*.
188) LXI = *Elidir*. GoM (3:17) = *Elidurus*.
189) As in GoM (3:17). LXI = *Alklyd*, present-day Dumbarton. It is from the ancient name of *Alklyd* that the modern name of Clyde has derived.

sick, and he sent messengers everywhere in all the realm to summon the nobility to come and visit him. And all of them having come to the town of Alclud, he commanded the door-keeper to allow them entry but one at a time, and [to tell them] to approach him quietly lest their noise should cause a pain in his head - which all believed.

And then Elidyr commanded his servants to arrest and behead any man who refused to swear loyalty to Arthal again, as they had done in time past. And so, when all of their vows were secured by consent and by threat, they were all reunited in peace with his brother. And Elidyr came to his brother at Eboracum, and he removed the crown from off his own head and placed it upon that of his brother, Arthal. And it was from that day that he was called Elidyr the Good.

And Arthal ruled as king for ten years, having repented his former sins. And ever after, he honoured the nobility, upheld truth in every place, did away with all cruelty, and bequeathed his riches to all. And he was buried at Carlisle.[190]

And Elidyr was once more raised to the throne. And his two younger brothers, Owen[191] and Peredur,[192] came to war against him with a mighty army. And they defeated and captured Elidyr, and took him to London where they threw him in prison and shared out the realm between themselves. To Owen fell all the land that lay west of the Humber, even Lloegria, Kymry and Cornwall. And Peredur's part was from the Humber to the north, even all of Albany. And when seven years were ended, Owen died, and all the realm fell into the hands of Peredur. And he governed the realm in [such] peace that none recalled his brother's reigns. And then Peredur died, and Elidyr was released from his captivity and was anointed king for the third time. And having passed all his [remaining] days in peace, he then died.

And after him, his son Gorbonianus[193] was crowned king, and he followed in his father's ways of justice and truth. And after him did Marganus,[194] the son of Arthal, rule, governing the realm in peace and concord. And after him, Einion,[195] his brother, took the crown. But he followed not his brother's ways

---

190) LXI = *kaelyl*, evidently a scribal error for *kaer lyl*, the city of Leil. GoM (3:17) states that Leicester was the city of his burial, doubtless misreading *kaer lyr* (Lear's city) for *kaer lyl* in the original source document.

191) LXI = *Owain*. GoM (3:18) = *Ingenius*.

192) LXI = *predyr*. GoM (3:18) = *Peredurus*.

193) As in GoM (3:19). GoM again seemingly misreads his text by stating that this king is an unnamed son of Gorbonianus. LXI states (perhaps correctly) that *Gorviniaw* is *Elidyr's* son. Later (see note 198), LXI states that *Gerennus* is *Geraint map Elidyr*.

194) As in GoM (3:19). LXI = *Morgan*.

195) As in LXI, which here has *Einon*. GoM (3:19) = *Ennianus*.

as king and was deposed in the sixth year [of his reign], for his cruelty and hatred of the truth entirely caused his downfall. And after him came Eidwal[196] as king, the son of Owen, his kinsman. And through dread of Einion's ruin, he ruled his people with justice. And then Run,[197] the son of Peredur, was anointed king. And after him Gerennus,[198] the son of Elidyr. Then Catellus,[199] his son, ruled the realm. And after Catellus did Coel[200] reign. And after Coel, Porrex. Then Cherin. And he, Cherin, had three sons, to wit Fulgenius, Edadus and Andragius,[201] and these three ruled the land the one after the other.

And after these, ruled Urien,[202] the son of Andragius. Then Eliud.[203] And then Cledaucus,[204] after whom came Cloten.[205] And he was followed by Gurgant.[206] Then Merianus.[207] And then Bladud[208] was made king. And after him came Cap,[209] and then Owen.[210] And after Owen, Sisillius.[211] And Beldgabred.[212] Then Arthmail,[213] his brother, became king. And Eidol,[214] and Redon,[215] and Rhydderch[216] [all ruled as king in their turn]. And then came the

---

196) As in LXI. GoM (3:19) = *Idvallo.*
197) LXI = *Rvn.* GoM (3:19) = *Runo.*
198) As in GoM (3:19). LXI = *Geraint.*
199) As in GoM (3:19). LXI = *Kadell.*
200) LXI = *Koel.* GoM (3:19) = *Millus.* It is impossible to say which is the misreading.
201) As in GoM (3:19). LXI = *ffylgniws, Eidal* and *Andras* respectively.
202) LXI = *Yrien.* GoM (3:19) = *Urianus.*
203) As in GoM (3:19). LXI = *Elvyrd.*
204) As in GoM (3:19). LXI = *Klydoc.*
205) LXI = *Klydno.* GoM (3:19) = *Clotenus.*
206) LXI = *Gorwst.* GoM (3:19) = *Gurgintius.*
207) As in GoM (3:19). LXI = *Mairiawn.*
208) LXI = *Blaiddyd.* GoM (3:19) = *Bledudo.* This is the second king to bear this name.
209) As in GoM (3:19). LXI = *Caff.*
210) LXI = *Owain.* GoM (3:19) = *Oenus.*
211) As in GoM (3:19). LXI = *Sayssyllt.* This is the third king to bear this name.
212) As in GoM (3:19). LXI = *Blegywyrd.* GoM calls him the "god of the minstrels".
213) LXI = *Arthmael.* GoM (3:19) = *Archmail.*
214) As in LXI. GoM (3:19) = *Eldol.*
215) As in GoM (3:19). LXI = *Rydion.*
216) As in LXI. GoM (3:19) = *Redechius.*

high and mighty Sawl.[217]

And after Sawl, Pirr[218] took the crown. And then Capoir.[219] And after him came Manogan,[220] his son, a most notable king who loved truth and justice. And then came Beli Mawr,[221] his son. And he reigned as king over Britain for forty years. And he had four sons, to wit Lud, Llefelys, Casswallon and Nennius.[222]

And of these, Lud was the firstborn, and upon his father's death he came to the throne. And he rebuilt the walls of London and encircled the city with farms. And he dwelt there the better part of each year. And within the city, he ordered the raising of many fine buildings such as were never seen in any land. And he called the city Caer Lud [after his own name], which city was later known as Caer Lundain, but after the coming of the Saxons, London.[223]

And Llefelys he loved above all his brothers for his wisdom and his eloquence. And when Llefelys had learned that the king of Gaul had died, leaving no heir but a daughter, and that she now ruled the kingdom, he advised his brother, Lud, to apply to the nobility of Gaul for the [hand of the] maiden [in marriage]. And straightway the damsel was given him, and with her the crown of the realm. And this he wore with righteousness all his days.

And after many years, three afflictions befell the island of Britain, such as had never been seen before.[224] The first was the coming of a people called the

---

217) LXI = *Sawl benn Ychel*. GoM (3:19) misreads his text by dividing this king's name into two. Latinizing *Sawl* as *Samuil* (misreading the w for *mui*) and *benn Ychel* as *Penissel*, he makes the fictitious *Penissel* to reign after *Samuil*, the mistake being further exasperated by misreading the Latin *cui samuil, cui penissel*. It is further confused by the *issel* element meaning 'humble' (perhaps an intended irony), and the *ychel* element meaning 'proud', for *Sawl benn Ychel* (or *Sawyl ben Uchel*) is listed in the Welsh Triads (23) as one of the three 'haughty' men of the island of Britain (*tri thrahauc enys prydein*).
218) As in LXI. GoM (3:19) = *Pir*.
219) As in GoM (3:19). LXI = *Kapeur*.
220) As in LXI. GoM (3:19) = *Digueillus*, a strange misreading on GoM's part.
221) As in LXI. GoM (3:20) = *Heli*.
222) LXI = *llydd, llefelys, Kasswallawn* and *Myniaw* respectively. GoM omits *Llefelys*.
223) Thus far GoM and LXI tally, except that GoM omits the following account of *Llefelys and the Three Plagues of Britain*. Was it missing from his copy of the source material? The strange story of *Llydd and Llefelys*, which now forms part of the Mabinogion, appears also in the *Brut y Brenhinnoedd* (or *Chronicle of the Kings*) in MS Llanstephan I.
224) The following account is entirely missing from all the Latin texts of GoM and many of the Welsh manuscripts.

Coritani,[225] whose knowledge was such that not a word could be whispered on the wind against them but that they knew of it. And thus could no harm befall them. And the second was a scream which, upon the eve of Beltain,[226] would rattle every hearth throughout Britain. And so fearfully did it cut through to the heart of man and beast, that men would wax pale and faint, and women would miscarry their unborn children. The youth of the land lost all their senses, and the beasts of the forest were struck barren by it. And the third was that all the food in Britain would go rotten unless it was consumed on the first night.

Now, whilst the first affliction was understood as to its cause, none knew the causes of the other two. And Lud was greatly troubled and vexed to see such afflictions befall the island of Britain. And so he prepared his fleet and went to see his brother, Llefelys. And when Llefelys learned of it, he came to greet him, and embraced him. And when Llefelys learned why he had come, he commanded a long tube to be made through which men could speak, and so the Coritani could not hear of their secret plans through their conversation. And they spoke [to each other] through the tube, but neither could hear anything but hissing and spluttering.[227] And Llefelys, suspecting that a sprite had got into the tube, commanded that it be flushed through with wine. And this cleansed the tube of the sprite. And then Llefelys gave to his brother a certain species of insect, and told him that on his return home, he was to mash the insects and dissolve them in cold water. And then he was to summon into one place the entire kingdom, both the Britons and the Coritani, and sprinkle all the people with the water. And this would kill the Coritani but do no harm to the Britons.

[And he said], "The second affliction in your realm, is the dragon of that island fighting with another dragon of a foreign land who seeks to conquer her. And the scream comes from your dragon out of anger and fear. And you may prove it in this manner," said he. "When you get home, measure the land from end to end, with its length and its breadth. And wheresoever you find the centre of the island to be, then there command a pit to be dug in the earth. And

---

225) LXI = *Koraniait*, a renegade British tribe not mentioned in GoM. Manley Pope (p. 177) adds: "The Coranians are said to have come from the country of Pwyl, and settled on the eastern coast of Britain, near the Humber, in the time of Lludd, and afterwards to have joined the Romans and Saxons against the Britons. Triads 41, 7 and 15 of *Welsh Archailogy*. They seem to have been the *Coritani* of the Roman writers, and to have given the name of Pwyl or Pool to several districts in Britain; viz. Welsh Pool, Pool in Cheshire and Dorsetshire, Liverpool, &c."

226) Mayday, a most important date in the pagan Celtic calendar.

227) LXI = *din dros benn*. 'Bottom instead of top,' or more familiarly, 'upside down.' It implies a confused noise or cacophony. Jones (1929) gives the amusing rendering, 'arsey-versey,' a mixture of 'arse upwards' and 'vice-versa.'

command that a great cauldron of beer, the finest to be had, be brought into the pit, and cover the cauldron with a cloth of satin. And you yourself must watch over these things. And you will hear the dragons warring fearfully in the air. And when they are exhausted with the battle, and have changed their form into that of swine, they will rest upon the cloth and drink the beer. And the cloth shall sink [under their weight] to the bottom of the cauldron, and there shall they fall asleep. And you must ensnare them in the cloth and bury them deep in the earth, even in the strongest cavern that can be found in all your realm. And whilst they are held there, no further affliction shall befall the island of Britain."

[And he said], "And the third affliction is caused by a mighty warlock who causes everyone to sleep, and carries away your food and drink. You must therefore [again] keep watch yourself and guard your provisions. And lest sleep overwhelms you, keep a bath of cold water nearby, and when drowsiness threatens, then plunge into the bath of water!"

And when Lud returned home, he summoned before him all the people of the realm. And he sprinkled the water upon each one, from which the Coritani died forthwith - but the Britons suffered no hurt. And straightway Lud commanded that all the island be measured in its length and its breadth. And the centre was found in Rydychen, [which is Oxford]. And there he commanded a great pit to be dug, even as Llefelys had counselled him. And there he discovered that all that his brother had told him was true. And when the pigs fell asleep, Lud wrapped them in the cloth. And beneath the Hill of Ambrosius,[228] in a stone chest, he buried them, deep inside the earth. And from that day, no more hideous scream was heard.

And the king commanded a great feast to be made. And when all was prepared, [he commanded] a trough of cold water to be placed near at hand. And so he watched the feast. And as he watched in this manner for most of the night, he heard the most beautiful music on earth lulling him to sleep. But he plunged himself into the water constantly. And he saw a great man clothed in mail enter [the chamber] with a large basket, and he watched him fill it with food and drink and [go to] make off with it. And Lud commanded him to stop, and said to him, "Though you have robbed me blind until now, you shall no longer do so - unless you are more powerful than I!"

And the dark one halted, and they fought so furiously that sparks flew from their swords. But Lud finally overcame the evil [one]. And the dark one cried the king mercy, saying that he would make good all the loss that he had caused him, and that henceforth he would be the king's true servant. And the king

---

228) LXI = dinas Emrys.

accepted his vow, and so did Lud make an end of all three afflictions.[229] And when he died, his body was buried in London near to the gate called Porth Llydd in the Old Welsh, but in Saxon, Ludgate.[230]

And he had two sons, Androgeus[231] and Tenvantius.[232] But because they were too young to rule the kingdom, Casswallon,[233] the son of Beli [Mawr], was anointed king. And Casswallon gave himself over to uphold truth and justice, and notwithstanding he was king, he sought no advantage over his nephews, but bestowed upon them large parts of the realm. He gave to Androgeus London and the earldom of Kent. And to Tenvantius he gave the earldom of Cornwall. But he, Casswallon, was king over all.

And in his days came Julius Caesar,[234] emperor of Rome, who was then conquering [diverse] lands.[235] And after he had conquered Gaul, from whence he espied the land of Britain, he enquired what land it was that lay opposite to him. And certain men told him that it was the island of Britain. And when Caesar perceived the greatness of the place, and what people they were who dwelt there, he said, "Men of Rome, those who dwell [in that land] are our kin, for the people of Rome and the Britons are both descended from Trojan stock. Aeneas, after the fall of Troy, was forefather to ourselves and to them. [Their] Brutus was the son of Silvius, [who was] the son of Ascanius, the son of Aeneas. And Brutus was the first to settle yonder island.[236] But I perceive that it will not be difficult for me to make yon island subject to the Senate of Rome. They are girt about with water, ignorant of warfare, the use of weapons and of

---

229) At this point the story takes up where it had earlier left off.
230) LXI = *lwyd gad*. Stow (p. 36) tells us that Ludgate was built ca 66 BC. It was considered one of the oldest gates of London.
231) As in GoM (3:20). LXI = *Afarwy*.
232) As in GoM (3:20). LXI = *Tenefan*. Also known to the Romans as *Tasciovanus*.
233) LXI = *Kasswallawn*. Julius Caesar (p. 110) knew him as Cassivelaunus, king of the *Catevellauni*.
234) LXI = *ilkassar*. The following account gives the Roman invasion of 55 BC as it was seen through the eyes of the Britons. A comparison between this account and that of Julius Caesar is given in *After the Flood* (see Bibliography), showing that LXI is not a mere rehash of Caesar's account.
235) LXI = *ynysoedd*, the plural of *ynys*, 'island', in this context embracing countries in general rather than islands in particular.
236) It is interesting that in his own account of the invasion, Julius Caesar states (p. 110) that the Britons claimed to be aboriginal. A version of the present chronicle, perhaps the original source material, must have been made known to him for him to have learned of the common ancestry of the Britons and Romans.

fighting.[237] But we must first send ambassadors to warn them not to resist the will of Rome, but to pay tribute, as have all other nations before them. And to do this without warfare, lest they should compel us to spill their blood who are our kin, and who trace their lineage [with us] to our forefather, Priam!"

And when Julius Caesar had sent these words, requiring Casswallon to do altogether according to his command, Casswallon deemed the demand a worthless thing, and sent a letter to Julius Caesar, saying this, "Greetings to Julius Caesar, tyrant of Rome, from Casswallon, king of the Britons, who tells him this - I marvel at the avarice of the people of Rome, how greatly they lust after silver and gold, inasmuch as they seek to impose tribute upon us who live on a sea-girt island on the edge of the world, for a land which until now we have freely possessed! Shame be upon you, O Caesar, and upon your command, for we alike are descended with you from the people of Aeneas Whiteshield. And for this reason, [if for no other], you should not ask of us eternal subjection. Wherefore know, O Caesar, that we shall fight for our country and our freedom rather than let you land here in Britain, should you now come across the sea as you have threatened!"[238]

And when Julius Caesar had read Casswallon's letter, and [had noted] his reply, he mustered a fleet and came to the mouth of the Thames.[239] And he was met [in battle] by Nennius,[240] Casswallon's brother, and Androgeus, his nephew, prince of London. Also Trahern,[241] earl of Cornwall, and Caradoc,[242] king of Albany, and by Gwerthaet, king of Gwent,[243] and also Brithael,[244] king of Dyfed. And straightway they, the Britons, made for the castle of Doral,[245] and

---

238) Again we hear the ring of authenticity in these sentiments. Contemporaries would have seen at first hand the policy of official greed which Caesar was eager to disguise in his own account.

239) LXI = *Temys*. The landing was actually at Walmer Beach, to the south of the Thames estuary.

240) As in GoM (4:3). LXI = *Nynniaw*.

241) LXI = *trahayant*.

242) LXI = *Kradawc*. GoM (4:3) = *Cridous*.

243) As in LXI. GoM (4:3) = *Gueithaet* of Venedotia.

244) As in LXI. GoM (4:3) = *Brithael* of Demetia.

245) As in LXI. GoM (4:3) = *Dorobellum*, as in Nennius (chap. 10). This fort was known later to the Romans as *Durolevum*, and lay between Rochester and Canterbury, an ideal gathering place for the British forces who did not know whether the Romans intended to march straight to London (Trinovantum) or along the south coast to present-day Sussex (then largely uninhabited) and thence north to London, thus avoiding the necessity of transporting an army across the Medway. It is most significant that Caesar displays no awareness of the fort or its name in his own account, which is a telling piece of evidence against the notion that the British account is a mere reworking of the Roman.

[from there] they came down to the shore. And they fought heroically on every side.

And Nennius and Caesar met [in battle], and Caesar lifted his sword to bring it down on Nennius' head. But he, Nennius, blocked it with his shield, so that the sword stuck fast in it. And he, Caesar, could not free it by virtue of the press of the soldiers about them. But when Nennius once took up his sword, then none could withstand its blows, for when the tribune, Labienus, came against Nennius, then straightway was he slain.[246] And so the best of Caesar's army were put to rout [by the Britons], whilst he himself was compelled to flee in disgrace back to Gaul.[247]

And the men of Gaul rebelled against him and gave him battle, and looked to overthrow his tyranny over them, for they supposed that his invasion of the Britons had come to nought because he had fled from them. And they heard also that Casswallon's ships were upon the sea to give him chase. But he, Caesar, pacified the people with a great sum of money to the princes of Gaul and liberty to all his captives.[248]

And after the victory, Casswallon came to London with all the nobility to pay homage to the gods. And after fifteen days Nennius died from his head wound, and he was buried with his sword near the north gate [of the city]. And the name of that sword was Red Death, for all who were struck by it were straightway slain.[249]

And in these days did Caesar build the castle of Odina, for fear that the men

---

246) LXI = *Alibiens*. Interestingly, the death of Alibiens is mentioned in Caesar's account, in which he appears as the tribune *Quintus Laberius Durus*. GoM (4:3) transposes the name understandably enough as *Labienus*, although Labienus (Caesar's second-in-command) had actually been left behind on the continent (Caesar, p. 108). Furthermore, Liberius was slain during the second attempt at invasion the following year in 54 BC according to Caesar, all of which indicates the sometimes garbled though authentic nature of the Celtic sources.
247) The remarkable contrast between the British and Roman accounts is seen in the complete omission from the British of all reference to British fighting tactics (compare Caesar, pp. 102-3 for a description of these). But then, as Flinders Petrie asks, why should they mention tactics which were all too familiar to themselves? Moreover, the British assessment of Caesar's hasty retreat to Gaul as a disgraceful flight is entirely accurate, but not an observation that finds any room in Caesar's own version of the events.
248) This is wholly borne out by Caesar's account.
249) GoM (4:4) has Yellow Death.

of Gaul might rise up against him a second time.[250] And at the end of two years, Caesar came a second time to wreak vengeance upon the Britons for his defeat.[251] And when Casswallon learned of it, he commanded that iron stakes, as stout as a man's thigh, should be planted in the Thames where Caesar's ships should come. And of a sudden they, the Romans, ran [their ships] upon the stakes and the ships were holed, drowning thousands of his men. And those who reached the banks were met by Casswallon and all the host of Lloegria. And Caesar fled to the shores of the Morani,[252] from whence he arrived at the castle of Odina.

And Casswallon came again to London where he gave a great feast for his nobles and servants. And there he made a sacrifice of thirty-two thousand animals of every sort. And they passed the nights in all manner of revelry. But a quarrel arose between two young princes whilst they were jousting. The one was called Hirlas, nephew to the king, and the other was Kyhylyn, nephew to Androgeus. And at the last, Kyhylyn slew Hirlas, the king's nephew, which thing caused a great uproar throughout the court. And the king was greatly

---

250) Caesar, significantly, doesn't name this fort. Flinders Petrie (p. 5) rightly suggests that the name reveals the genuine though garbled nature of the British intelligence reports, for Caesar does state that he sent troops to Lisieux (Lexovii) on his return to Gaul, and that the name of the river, Olina, there (which again Caesar doesn't give) suggests the origin of [G]odinae. Manley Pope (pp. 181-2) adds: "Odnea, Odna, Dodres. The latter points to the Tour d'Ordre; Turris Ordans, or Ordensis of Boulogne, said to have been built for a lighthouse by Caligula [it was the site where Caligula ordered his troops to gather seashells as plunder from Neptune - see Suetonius, p. 177]; and probably on the site of the fort, or rampart constructed by Caesar, when pressed by the Morini, in the year previous to the first invasion of Britain. In this history [i.e. the Welsh Chronicle] and in the account of Caesar's invasions, as given by Nennius, Bede, Giraldus Cambrensis, and the author of the *Flores Historiarum*, the general circumstances of the narrative are the same, even to the names of *Androgeus* and *Labienus*. These accounts differ widely from that given by Caesar himself in his *Commentaries*, as to prove decisively that they were not of Roman but of British origin. The differences between the British and Roman narratives are such as might havebeen found between the Carthaginian and Roman histories of the Punic Wars, had the former ever appeared. In Caesar's narrative of his second invasion, he has, if the British historians be correct, so connected the events of two distinct invasions, (by wholly omitting his having been defeated and forced to return to France, and induced by the treachery of some of the Britons, made a second attempt with more success,) as to make the whole seem to be the transactions of one and the same invasion."
251) In fact, it was only one year later. Were the Britons counting inclusively?
252) Another interesting example of this invasion being seen through the eyes of the Britons. Caesar (p. 110) tells us that to safeguard his ships, he had them hauled out of the water and taken some way inland into camp, a prodigious feat of engineering of which the Romans were quite capable. Not suspecting this capability, the Britons heard from their scouts that the Roman ships were gone from the beach, and they thus supposed - understandably enough - that the Romans had fled once again.

angered, and he desired to bring the nephew of Androgeus before the jurisdiction of his court. But Androgeus thought it ill-done, saying that in London alone could atonement be made for all offences done in the realm - which he was willing to do. But the king wanted nothing save to have Kyhylyn in his power, which Androgeus refused, knowing well the king's intentions. And Androgeus left the court and went back to his own estates.

And when the king saw this, he pursued him with a mighty host and utterly laid waste the land with fire and the sword. But it availed him nothing, and Androgeus wondered how he might overcome the king. And he was counselled to send to Caesar and say that he would help him if he came again to Britain, and he would help him in his invasion and submit all Britain to Caesar's will.[253] And as a token of his pledge, Androgeus sent him Conan, his [own] son, and thirty-two others as hostages from among the princes of the island of Britain.[254]

And so Caesar gathered a fleet and came ashore at the port of Richborough, where Androgeus welcomed him with honour.[255] And at this time was Casswallon the king laying siege to London. But when Casswallon learned of Caesar's coming [again] to Britain, he prepared to come against him. And when he had come to a wooded valley near to Canterbury, he espied the Roman encampment.[256] And they did battle in that place, and there was great bloodshed on either side. And at last the Britons were driven back to a high hill-fort, which they stoutly defended and slew many of the men of Rome. And on seeing this, the Romans surrounded the hill-fort, intending to starve the Britons [into submission]. And so Casswallon sent to Androgeus, and besought him to make peace between himself and Caesar.[257]

And Androgeus was astonished, and said, "It is not to be wondered at that he should seek a truce who is a lion in peace, but a [mere] lamb in war!" But then Androgeus stood before Caesar and spoke to him these words, "I promised you, my lord, the submission of all Britain. And behold, here it is if you will but have Casswallon to be under you as king and pay tribute to the Senate of

---

253) Androgeus (LXI = *Afarwy*), here identified as the British traitor known to Caesar (p. 113) as *Mandubracius*. The name *Mandubracius* is the Latinized form of the British *Du bradwr*, or *Mandubrad*, which means 'Black' or 'Filthy Traitor.' Doubtless Afarwy, i.e. Androgeus, had been introduced to Caesar by the Gaulish Celts under this term, and Caesar, or his secretary, had assumed that it was his proper name. What Afarwy thought whenever he heard Caesar address him by this title is not recorded.
254) GoM (4:9) states thirty hostages.
255) LXI = *Rwydom*. Latin *Rutupi Portus* = Richborough.
256) LXI = *kaer gaint*. Did Kasswallawn return to the fort of Doral (Durolevum)? This seems likely. GoM (4:9) calls the woody glen the "valley of Durobernia".
257) Caesar (p. 114) informs us that the message arrived via Commus, a British envoy.

Rome." But Caesar scorned the proposition, and on perceiving this Androgeus said, "Though I surely undertook to submit to you the island of Britain, I did not promise you the slaughter of my own people. For they have not rendered me so much harm that it cannot be healed, and I will not consent to the murder of my people!"

And so Caesar made a pact with Casswallon upon his paying to the Senate of Rome for the island of Britain three thousand pounds each year.[258] And upon this being ratified, they came together to London and made their winter-quarters there.[259] And the summer following, Caesar returned to Rome and Androgeus with him, to come against Pompey[260] who in those days was [seeking to] rule the empire there. And Casswallon continued to rule the land of Britain for [a further] seven years.[261] And when he died, he was buried at Eboracum. And after Casswallon, Tenvantius, the son of Lud, was made king.

And after Tenvantius, Cymbeline[262] was made king whom Caesar had raised [as his own son]. And Cymbeline loved the people of Rome more than any other, so he was willing to pay to them the tribute [promised by Casswallon]. And in his days Christ Jesus was made man. And when Cymbeline had reigned for twelve years,[263] he had two sons, [the one named] Guiderius,[264] and [the other] Arvirargus.[265]

And upon Cymbeline's death, Guiderius was anointed king. And when he thought himself safe upon the throne, he stopped the [flow of] tribute to the men of Rome. And when the Romans learned of it, they sent Claudius Caesar[266] and a mighty host with him to the land of Britain. And when the emperor came

---

258) Intriguingly, Caesar omits the size of the tribute from his own account, because in the event he received nothing from the Britons.

259) Caesar makes no mention of quartering in London that winter, only that he returned with his army to Gaul. Lucan's *Pharsalia* (II,572) makes the jibe that Caesar had "...run away in terror from the Britons whom he had come to attack!" That this was said by a Roman is a most telling point.

260) LXI = *Pontenis*, the British form of Pompey (*Gnaeus Pompeius Magnus*), Julius Caesar's opponent in the civil war.

261) GoM (4:11) has six years.

262) LXI = *Kynvelyn*, otherwise (Shakespeare's) Cymbeline, or Cunobelinus.

263) GoM (4:12) has ten years.

264) As in GoM (4:12). LXI = *Gwydr*.

265) As in GoM (4:12). LXI = *Gwairydd*. GoM, pointing out how feared and respected Arvirargus was to become among the Romans, cites the Roman poet Juvenal (I, iv, 126-7) : "Regem aliquem capies aut de themone Britanno decidet Arvirargus." - "...either you will capture a certain king, or else Arvirargus will tumble from the British chariot pole!"

266) LXI = *Eloywkassar*.

ashore, he besieged Portchester[267] and assaulted the castle [there]. But when he could not prevail, he sealed up the city gates with great stones to enclose the people therein, that they might die of hunger. And when Guiderius heard of it, he assembled a mighty army, and on coming to Portchester he fell upon the men of Rome. And a far greater number were slain by his hand than by the rest of his army together.

And then came Hamon the Betrayer,[268] who, from the hostages among the Britons at Rome, had learned the [Britons'] tongue. And he cast off his own armour and donned that of a Briton who had been slain, and he mingled amongst the [British] warriors. And when he could, he slew the king and wormed his way back amongst the host to his own army. And then he cast aside that armour, and put on his own again. And when Arvirargus had heard of his brother's death, he threw off his apparel and put on his brother's kingly armour, and exhorted his warriors to fight heroically and put the men of Rome to flight. And Hamon, along with the greater part of his host, fled to the place called Porth Hamon, or Porth Hamwnt[269] as it is called to this day, and there was Hamon slain.

And from there came Arvirargus to that place where Claudius Caesar was besieging Portchester. And when the garrison within the castle knew that the Britons were coming to their aid, they sallied forth from the castle to do battle with the men of Rome. And many died on either side. And yet, due to the [overwhelming] number of the Romans, they, the men of Rome, took the castle and drove Arvirargus headlong to Winchester. And Claudius Caesar followed with his army and hoped to entrap the Britons until they should die of hunger. But when Arvirargus perceived this, he mustered his soldiers and sallied out. And when Claudius Caesar saw this, he sent to the Britons and sued for peace. And straightway peace was made between them. And to ratify that peace, Claudius Caesar betrothed his daughter to Arvirargus.

And afterwards, with the strength of the Britons [to help them], the men of Rome brought the Orkneys and other islands into subjection. And when the winter was past, the girl, the daughter of Claudius, [who was] without peer for her grace and beauty, came from Rome, and Arvirargus wedded her. And then Claudius Caesar built a city which he named Gloucester[270] on the banks of the Severn [where lies] the border between Kymry and Lloegria.

---

267) LXI = *kaer beris*, Portchester.
268) GoM (4:12) = *Lelius Hamo*.
269) Southampton.
270) LXI = *kaer loyw*, lit. the city of Claudius.

55

And in those days did Christ suffer at Jerusalem, and Peter the Apostle was made bishop of Antioch,[271] from whence he came to Rome as bishop. And he sent Mark to Egypt[272] as its teacher and evangelist, to preach the Gospel which he, Mark, had written himself.

And when he was able, Claudius Caesar returned to Rome and left the rule of Britain to Arvirargus. And when he, Claudius Caesar, had departed the realm, Arvirargus took on rashness and pride, and withheld the tribute to the men of Rome. And when Claudius Caesar had learned of this, he sent Vespasian[273] with a mighty host to exact tribute from the land of Britain. And when his fleet was fully manned, they came ashore at the port of Richborough.[274] And Arvirargus and his host withstood them and foiled their landing. They therefore set sail and came ashore at Totnes. And after disembarking, they besieged Exeter[275] and assaulted it.

And when the king learned of this, he mustered his army and arrived there at the close of the seventh day, and attacked the men of Rome, doing battle against them. And the following day, so large was the multitude of Romans that it was hard [for Arvirargus] to overcome them. But then came the queen[276] to make peace between them, and they arrived together at London whence they sent out joint forces to conquer Ireland.[277] And when winter was past, Vespasian returned to Rome. But he [first] bound Arvirargus by vows [of obedience to rule peacefully] in Britain till the end of his days. And at his death, he, Arvirargus, was laid to rest in [the precincts of] the temple in Gloucester which Claudius Caesar had built.

And after Arvirargus did Marius[278] his son become king. And in his days

---

271) LXI = *anossia*, referring to Peter's apostolic office at Antioch, a synchronism which would place these events in the decade AD33 - 43.

272) LXI = *Eifft*.

273) LXI = *Vassbassian*. Vespasian held the command of the II Augusta legion.

274) LXI = *porth rydipi*.

275) LXI = *kaer benhwylgoed*.

276) GoM (4:16) names her as *Genvissa*.

277) LXI = *Iwerddon*. There is no mention of Vespasian going to Ireland in any Roman account, although like his successor, Agricola, he may well have entertained the idea and boasted of its possibilities in the hearing of certain Britons. A more probable explanation, however, lies in the confusion between the Latin *Hibernia* - Ireland - and *hibernus* meaning winter-quarters, (hence our word *hibernate*). Vespasian may simply have been talking about setting up his winter-quarters rather than invading Ireland. It is a mistake that an early Briton, as yet unfamiliar with the more subtle nuances of Latin, could easily have made, but not a medieval Latin-speaking forger.

278) As in GoM (4:17). LXI = *Mayric*.

came Soderic,[279] the king of the Picts, from Ireland[280] with a mighty host to Albany, and conquered it. And on learning of this, he, Marius, came forth against him and did battle with him, and caused him to flee. And Soderic was slain as he fled. And Marius apportioned to them, the Picts, a part of Albany in which to dwell. But when they had settled the land, the Picts had no womenfolk, and they came to the Britons to ask for their daughters as wives. But the Britons deemed it imprudent to grant them to them, and so the Picts went abroad to Ireland and took Gaelic women[281] for their wives, and from these are the Scots descended.

And when Marius had secured the kingdom, of his own free will and pleasure he sought accord with the men of Rome. And he established new laws throughout his kingdom and reigned in peace for as long as he lived. And when Marius died, so Coel[282] his son was made king. He had been brought up at Rome, and such was his love for Rome that though he could easily have done so, he did not withhold the tribute whilst he lived.

And after Coel, Lucius[283] his son took the crown. And his temperament was like that of his father. And when he was firmly established as king, he sent to Eleutherus,[284] the bishop of Rome, to beseech him that he might send teachers of Christ to Britain, to the end that, by their teaching and preaching, he [and his people] might take on the faith of Christ.[285] And he, Eleutherus, sent him two such teachers, Duvianus and Faganus,[286] and they preached to him of Christ's Incarnation, cleansing him in holy and true baptism and all his kingdom with him.

And then Lucius closed down the temples that had been raised for [the worship of] false gods, and commanded that they be dedicated anew in the name

---

279) As in GoM (4:17). LXI = *Rodric*.

280) LXI = *sseithia*. This is thought by some to mean Scandinavia, but the context points very clearly to Ireland (*Scotia*, a variant of *Scythia*). The Irish named Scythia as their earlier country of origin.

281) LXI = *Gwyddylessav*, lit. Goidelic women.

282) LXI = *Koel*. GoM (4:18) = *Coilus*.

283) As in GoM (4:19). LXI = *Iles*.

284) LXI = *Elenteriws*, Pope Eleutherus. According to the *Annuario Pontifico*, Eleutherus was pope from AD 175-189. According to *Liber Pontificalis*, Lucius sent to Rome for teachers in ca AD 180.

285) Christianity had been brought to Britain long before Lucius, as is shown by Origen and Tertullian, the latter of whom tells us that parts of Britain which were inaccessible to the Romans, had already been subdued by Christ.

286) As in GoM (4:19). LXI = *Dyfan* and *ffagan*. They are otherwise known as *Fugatius* and *Damianus*, of whom Platina wrote in 1479 (see Flinders Petrie, p. 12).

of Almighty God and the saints. And he placed in them diverse orders of priests to live in them and pay homage to God. And there were in those days sixty-eight dioceses[287] in the land of Britain, and three archbishoprics that governed them all. And these were in the three chief cities of the realm, to wit London, and Eboracum, and Caerleon-on-Usk. And when the land was divided between the three archbishoprics, then to that of Eboracum was added Deira and Bernicia,[288] as well as all [the land] north from the Humber.

And to the archbishopric of London was given all Lloegria and Cornwall, as bounded by the Severn, And to that of Caerleon-on-Usk was given Kymry from the Severn onwards, because Caerleon was supreme over the other two. And henceforth the king made over to them large grants of land. And at Gloucester he died, being buried in the abbey there one hundred and thirty-six years after the birth of Christ.[289]

And in those days there were in Britain twenty-eight [pagan] temples, with three other temples over them, and the lands of the temples were under the jurisdiction of the three. And to each of these [pagan] temples was appointed a [Christian] bishop. And to each of the three ruling temples, there was appointed an archbishop in the three cities aforementioned.

Now, because Lucius had no heir, there arose unrest between the Britons and Rome, and Rome lost authority [amongst the Britons] from that day on. And when the Senate of Rome were told this, they sent Severus,[290] a senator of Rome, with a contingent of twenty thousands soldiers.[291] And he generally subdued the Britons, some of whom fled with their leader Sulgenius[292] through Deira and Bernicia. And there were many skirmishes between them to the consternation of the emperor. And he commanded a wall to be built between Deira and Albany at the expense of the people [of Britain] from sea to sea, so that it would be easier to withstand those Britons [under Sulgenius].

And when Sulgenius had perceived that neither he nor the Britons [under him] could fight the Romans to advantage, he went across to Ireland in search of help. And when he had recruited all the young warriors of that land, he returned to Britain and laid siege to Eboracum and assaulted it. And as news of

---

287) GoM (4:19) states that there were twenty-eight 'archflamens' or dioceses in Britain.
288) LXI = *deifyr* and *brynaich*, the ancient kingdoms of Deira and Bernicia.
289) This date is patently wrong. GoM (5:1) tries to correct it to the year AD 156, but even this is wrong. The errors are doubtless due to a defaced or damaged original.
290) As in GoM (5:2). LXI = *sseferys*.
291) GoM (5:2) states two legions.
292) As in GoM (5:2). LXI = *ssilien*.

it travelled throughout the land, so most of the Britons abandoned the Roman emperor, and defected to Sulgenius. And straightway Severus marched with his army to do battle with Sulgenius, and Sulgenius mortally wounded him. And Severus died from that wound[293] and was buried in Eboracum.

And Severus had two sons, [the one named] Bassian,[294] and [the other] named Geta.[295] And the mother of Geta was of Roman descent, but Bassian's mother was a Briton. And after the death of his father, Severus, the Romans made Geta their appointee because his mother's lineage was of Rome. And so the Britons chose Bassian for their king, because his mother's lineage was of Britain. And thus discord arose between the brothers. And on a certain day they came together, and at that meeting Geta was slain and Bassian won the kingdom for himself.

And in those days there lived in Britain a certain youth named Carausius.[296] And though he was low-born, he was renowned for his resolve which had been seasoned through many battles. And he went to Rome and asked the senators of Rome to grant him a fleet with which to defend the island of Britain against the foreign invader[297] - from which he promised much would be gained. And so he returned to the land of Britain and increased the strength of the country. And he put to sea and visited many ports, causing great suffering in the neighbouring lands [by] destroying them, murdering and burning.

And all who traded in violence and piracy came to him, so that he soon had such numbers who followed him that he feared no man. And seeing how everything prospered him, he sent to the Britons to see if they would have him for their king. And if they would, he would destroy the men of Rome and cleanse the land of them, and deliver the Britons from the hand of the foreign invader, the Picts.

And having won his desire, he went with a mighty host against Bassian, the Romans and the Picts. And the Picts turned on the Romans in the very first battle, and in that engagement was Bassian slain. And the Romans were compelled to flee, for they knew not who were for them or who were against them. And when Carausius had won the day through the treachery of the Picts,

---

293) According to GoM (5:2), Sulgenius also dies in this battle.
294) As in LXI. GoM (5:2) = *Bassianus*.
295) As in GoM (5:2). LXI = *Getta*.
296) As in GoM (5:3). LXI = *Karan*.
297) lit. 'alien nation,' in this case the Picts. The Saxons also fall under this title from the early 4th century onwards.

he handed Scotland to them, in which they are yet to be found in that part called Prydyn.[298]

And on learning of this, the Senate of Rome sent Allectus,[299] a Roman senator, to Britain, with three legions of soldiers. And Carausius and his army fell upon them and attacked them, and in that first battle was Carausius slain. And Allectus wreaked havoc amongst the Britons, and they bewailed their misfortune and elected Asclepiodotus[300] to lead them, for he was earl of Cornwall. And he descended upon Allectus who was holding a feast to his gods in London.

And when Allectus beheld him coming, he mustered his troops and engaged the Britons in the midst of great bloodshed. But at last the Romans fled the field and the Britons pursued them, and slew them in their thousands. And Allectus was slain also, and the Romans closed the gates of London against the Britons. And Livius Gallus,[301] who was Allectus' colleague, took over the command of the Roman [garrison]. But Asclepiodotus invested the city and sent to all the princes of Britain, telling them that he was besieging London.

And he commanded all to come to him quickly and help him. And upon his command there straightway came the men of South Wales, the men of North Wales and the men of Albany.[302] And when all were set down before the city, they battered down the walls, going through them and over them [into the city]. And they began to slaughter the Romans. And when they, the Romans, beheld this, they sent to the king and besought his protection, that he should let them leave [the city] and return alive to their own land. But whilst the king was being counselled concerning them, the men of Gwynedd[303] fell upon the Romans and

---

298) Corresponding roughly to present-day Argyle.
299) As in GoM (5:4). LXI = *Alectys*.
300) As in GoM (5:4). LXI = *Alyssglapitwlws*. This king is also referred to by Bede (1:6), who rather oddly calls him the Prefect of the Praetorian Guard. Asclepiodotus was, in fact, the British petty king of Cornwall whom the Britons elected to lead the nation in battle.
301) As in GoM (5:4). LXI = *Boiysgalys*.
302) LXI = *Allan*, evidently a misreading for Alban.
303) GoM (5:4) = *Venedoti*.

slew them every one.[304]

And after these things, Asclepiodotus took the crown and ruled the kingdom for twenty years.[305] And in his days began the persecution which Diocletian,[306] emperor of Rome, instigated against the Christians, almost wiping out the Christian faith. And then came Maxen and Herculius, two noblemen of Rome,[307] at the command of that wicked one, Diocletian, and pulled down the churches, burned the books of the Bible, and murdered the Christians both laymen and clergy. And in those days were slain Saint Alban of Verulamium,[308] and Aaron of Chester,[309] his fellow [in martyrdom]. And then arose Coel,[310] earl of Gloucester, and he fought against Asclepiodotus and straightway slew him.

And then Constans,[311] a senator of Rome who had been subduing Spain, came [with his host] to Britain to make war against Coel. But, having named the day upon which battle was to be given, they suddenly made peace. And when but a month and a week had passed by, Coel died. And he had held the crown for ten years.[312]

And Constans took Helen[313] as his wife, [she being] the only daughter of

304) GoM (5:4) adds the information that the massacre took place beside a brook in the city called in the British tongue *Nantgallum*. The later Saxons knew the stream as the *Galabroc*, and modern Londoners know it as the *Walbrook*, which lies to the east of St Paul's Cathedral. *Nant* means a steam or brook in Old Welsh, and the *gallum* element preserves the name of *Livius Gallus* (also preserved in *Galabroc*) who commanded the Roman garrison of London after the death of Allectus. In the 16th century, Stow (p. 108) in common with historians ever since, dismissed the account as a fable. However, the Walbrook was covered over in the 19th century, but before this work took place the bed of the stream was excavated in the 1860s by Colonel Pitt-Rivers and others. They found a very large number of skulls that had once formed a large heap of human heads. Some of these skulls are preserved today in the Museum of London, and their presence beneath the Walbrook (which neither Geoffrey of Monmouth nor the Welsh chronicler can have known anything about in the 12th century) is telling evidence for the original record's authenticity (see also Thorpe, p. 19).

305) GoM (5:5) states ten years, suggesting a damaged text.

306) LXI = *Diaklassiawn*, emperor of Rome from AD 284-305. His persecution of the Church was inaugurated in AD 303 and lasted until his retirement two years later.

307) *Maxen* and *Erkwlff*. Maximus Herculius was, in fact, one man, not two. Bede (1:6) calls him simply *Herculius*. GoM gives his name correctly.

308) LXI = *Virolan*, modern St Albans.

309) LXI = *Aron kaer llion*. Bede (1:7) and Gildas (chap. 10) agree with Chester.

310) LXI = *Koel*, the Old King Cole of the nursery rhyme. LXI correctly gives his city as Gloucester (*Kaer loyw*), whereas GoM (5:6) states that he was of Colchester which only became his centre of operations during his later rebellion against Rome.

311) LXI = *Konstans*. GoM (5:6) = *Constantius*.

312) GoM (5:6) omits the length of his reign.

313) As in GoM (5:6). LXI = *Elen lyddawc*.

Coel. And she was surnamed Helen the Fair, for such beauty of face and figure had never before been seen. And a son was born to them whose name was Constantine,[314] the son of Constans. And this is he who wrested Rome from [the hands of] Maxen the Cruel,[315] he and his three uncles, his mother's brothers, who were called Ioelinus, Trahern and Marius.[316]

And Trahern came with three armies to free Britain from [the tyranny of] Octavius,[317] earl of Erging and Eyas. And he, Trahern, took Kaer Beris [which is Portchester]. And at the close of the second day [of fighting], Octavius approached the field of battle,[318] close to Winchester, and won his first victory there. And Trahern was driven headlong to his ships, coming ashore in Albany so that he might renew the fight [against Octavius]. And Trahern defeated Octavius across the land until he, Octavius, sought refuge in Lochland and asked for help from Gunbert,[319] king of Prydyn, in bringing about the downfall of Trahern. And so the Earl of the Mighty Fortress, Gunbert, lay in wait for Trahern with a hundred mounted knights in a vale through which he, Trahern, must pass. And when Trahern arrived [in that place], he, Gunbert, slew him.

And so Octavius won the crown of Britain and ruled the kingdom. And he grew mighty in riches and assembled a great host of warriors, horses, weapons and the trappings [of war], so that no king could easily contest him [in battle]. And thus did Octavius hold on to his crown until the days in which two emperors came to rule at Rome, [whose names were] Gracianus and Valentinianus.[320] And he ruled the land of Britain almost to the end of his days. But lacking a [male] heir, and having none other but an only daughter, he summoned [to council] all the nobility of Britain to discuss with them the governance of the realm, and how [and to whom] he might best marry his daughter Helen.[321] And certain [of his nobles] advised him [in council] to bestow his kingdom upon his nephew, his brother's son Conan, [surnamed] Mairiadawc,[322] and to wed his daughter to the prince of some other land along

---

314) As in GoM (5:6). LXI = *Kystemim*, evidently an error for *Kystennin*.
315) GoM (5:7) = *Maxentius* - the dictator, *Maxentius Pius Felix Invictus*, who ruled 306-13.
316) As in GoM (5:8). LXI = *Llywelyn*, *Trahaern* and *Mayric* respectively.
317) LXI = *Eydaf*. GoM (5:8) = *Octavius*, prince of the *Gewissei*.
318) LXI = *Maes Vrien*. GoM (5:8) = *Maisuria*.
319) As in GoM (5:8). LXI = *Gyttbert*. Curiously, GoM translates *Prydyn* here as Norway.
320) As in GoM (5:8). LXI = *Grassiant* and *Afalawnt*.
321) GoM doesn't name Octavius' daughter.
322) LXI = *Kynan Mairiadawc*. GoM (5:9) = *Conanus Meridiadocus*.

with a portion of this land's wealth [as a dowry for her]. And others counselled him that she should be betrothed to a prince of this land, and the crown with her.

And then spoke Caradoc,[323] earl of Cornwall, saying, "Now are we subject to the will of Rome. And my counsel therefore is this, that you send to Rome, telling them that you have chosen Maximianus,[324] who is the son of Ioelinus, the uncle of Helen the Fair, and whose mother was the daughter of a Roman senator, to receive your kingdom and your daughter [as his wife]. And this will earn the assent of the Senate of Rome, and they will help us to defend our land against the foreign invader."

But on this [advice] they, the council, hesitated. And upon this, the earl Caradoc sent his son Mayric[325] to Rome. Now it was a rare thing for there to be any accord between the Romans and those of other lands, and when Mayric observed their discord, he said to Maximianus, " I marvel that you tolerate these people!" "Then what should I do?" asked Maximianus. "Come with me," said Mayric, "to the land of Britain, and marry Helen, the daughter of Octavius the king of Britain, and with her possess the kingdom also. And so, by the might of the Britons, you may conquer any land that resists you."

And this pleased Maximianus, and he gathered a fleet and sailed to Gaul, and compelled them to obey him and give him gold and silver. And word was brought to the king of the Britons that a fleet had put to sea but that it was unknown where it might come to land. And so Octavius commanded all the young warriors of Britain to defend the realm against the foreign invader. And Conan, with a mighty army, came to the hill of Kent [at Dover]. And when Maximianus beheld the magnitude of the host awaiting him, he hurried straightway to Mayric, and said, "That army is prepared to meet us, and wise counsel must be had if we are to face them!"

And so were elected twelve of the eldest and wisest men, and these were put ashore in a boat.[326] And they each carried in their hands as a sign of their peaceful intent, a green olive branch. And they came before Conan Mairiadawc and saluted him courteously, and told him that they were ambassadors of Maximianus to the king of the Britons. And Conan asked [them], "If he, Maximianus, comes in peace, then what needs he with such a mighty host as that?" And they answered, "Lest he should be assaulted upon his journey." And when Conan perceived their true mission, he wished to do battle lest he should

---

323) LXI = *Kradawc*. GoM (5:9) = *Caradocus*.
324) As in GoM (5:9). LXI = *Maxen Wledic*.
325) LXI = *Mayryc*. GoM (5:9) = *Mauricius*.
326) According to GoM, they came ashore at Southampton.

lose his crown. But Caradoc, earl of Cornwall, counselled him with these words, "Let these men go on to the king, and let him decide what should be done with them."

Then they, the ambassadors, went to the castle at Caernarvon,[327] where Octavius and his daughter Helen held their court. And straightway Maximianus took Helen for his wife, and the rule of the kingdom with her. And on hearing of it, Conan went to Albany and raised a mighty army there, and descended past the Humber and began to lay waste the country. And then Maximianus came and caused them to flee, and Conan returned the second time with his host, and peace was wrought between them, that they should stand or fall together. And afterwards, at the close of the fifth year, Maximianus and Conan invaded Gaul where Himbaldus[328] the king did rule. And there they slew him. And so to Conan Mairiadawc did Maximianus speak these words, "Because I deprived you of the land of Britain, I shall bestow Armorica upon you!"

And this was the first occasion upon which Britons came to Armorica,[329] and from that day to this it has been called Brittany. And from thence did Maximianus march, even to the city of Rennes[330] in Normandy. And in fear of him the Gauls fled [the place], leaving the castles and the cities [to stand] empty. And from there, Maximianus went to Rome and made war against Gracianus and Valentinianus, emperors of Rome, and he straightway slew the one and chased away the other from Rome.[331]

And in those days there were many battles between the Britons of Armorica and the Gauls.

And when it had been this way for many years, the men of Armorica, wishing to obtain proper wives, sent envoys to the land of Britain, even to the earl of Cornwall,[332] who ruled as vicegerent in the realm. And they besought him to send to Conan Mairiadawc eleven thousand damsels of noble descent in the land, with their attendants, and sixty virgins[333] of base family. And when this number of women had been gathered, they set out in ships. But whilst at

---

327) LXI = *arvon*.
328) As in GoM (5:12). LXI = *Hymblat*. GoM states fifteen thousand were killed with him.
329) LXI = *llydaw*. The migration to Brittany (Armorica) also appears in Gildas (13 & 14).
330) As in GoM (5:13). LXI = *Roam*.
331) Gracianus (r. 367-383), or Gratian, was co-emperor with Valentinian (375-392 - see also note 342) and Theodosius, who ruled the eastern part of the empire. As LXI says, Gracianus was indeed slain in battle by Maximianus (Magnus Maximus), in August 383 at Lyons.
332) GoM (5:15) names the earl as *Dionotus*.
333) GoM (5:16) states sixty thousand others of a lower rank. LXI is probably the accurate version.

sea, a contrary wind arose and scattered the ships to different places, and some of them sank.

And there were in those days warring on the seas against the men of Germany, under the command of Gracianus,[334] emperor of Rome, Wanius and Melga.[335] And these encountered two ships full of women which had been drifting upon the sea of Gaul. And when they learned from the women that the land of Britain lay open [and undefended], they set sail for Britain. And this Wanius was lord of the Huns,[336] and Melga was king of the Poitevins.[337] And after they landed in Albany, they slew the people [of the land] wherever they went. And when this came to the ears of Maximianus in Rome, he sent two legions of soldiers, with Gracianus to command them,[338] to defend the land of Britain. And there was war between them and the invaders, with multitudes slain on either side. And Wanius and Melga were driven headlong into Ireland.

And Maximianus was slain in those days at Rome along with all the Britons who had come [to that place with him], save those who fled on foot to Armorica. And when Gracianus had learned of the death of Maximianus, he usurped the crown of Britain for himself, and lorded it over the Britons with great cruelty for many years. And in the end he was slain by his own men. And when Wanius and Melga received knowledge of the slaying of Gracianus, they gathered an army from among the men of Lochland, Danes, Scots and Picts, and arriving in Britain they put the land to the flame and the sword from coast to coast, slaying multitudes [in their wake].

And when the Britons saw that they could not succeed in overcoming them, they sent to Rome for help. And they received a legion of soldiers with Severus[339] as commander over them. And as they reached the land of Britain, they engaged the enemy and drove them from its shores. And then, as agreed by all, they built a stone wall between Deira and the north, that the foreign invader might not oppress them so easily in future days.

And upon their arrival in London, the Romans commanded Guithelinus[340] to proclaim that the Romans had sacrificed both their fighters and their fortune in the defence of Britain, more than they had ever received from the Britons [in

---

334) As Gracianus was slain by this time, perhaps this refers to an earlier commission of his.
335) As in GoM (5:16). LXI = *Gwnwas* and *Melwas*.
336) LXI = *brenhin hinawd*, i.e. king of the Huns.
337) LXI = *Paittio*, i.e. of Poitou or Poitiers.
338) LXI = *Grassian*. This is obviously not the Gracianus who was previously slain. In the Latin text of GoM, he is *Gracianus municeps*, the same Gratian who appears in Bede (1:11).
339) LXI = *Sefervys*. GoM (6:1) doesn't actually name Severus.
340) As in GoM (6:2), who tells us that he was archbishop of London. LXI = *Kyhylyn*.

tribute], and that from that day they would no more labour to defend it.[341] And the people mourned loudly when they saw their allies deserting them. And so the Romans took ship and returned to their own land.

And when Wanius and Melga had learned of this, they mustered the greatest army that they could and invaded Albany. And they warred against the Britons and slew them, and subdued Albany as far as the Humber and continually assaulted them. And when the Britons perceived that they could not resist their foes, they raised a pitiful cry to Aetius,[342] the emperor of Rome, beseeching him to help them fight off their enemies.[343] But when the Senate of Rome received their petition, they disdained it utterly, and from that day on they, the Romans, renounced the land of Britain and disowned its tribute. And the Britons, having learned of their renunciation by the men of Rome, sent Guithelinus, archbishop of London, to Armorica to seek help from Aldroenus,[344] king of Armorica, who was the fourth to reign [there] after Conan Mairiadawc. And when Guithelinus had informed the king of the despair of the Britons because of the foreign invader, the king was moved and allotted them two thousand mounted knights with Constantine[345] his brother to lead them. And when the fleet was prepared, they set sail for the land of Britain and came ashore in Lloegria at Totnes. And when Wanius and Melga learned of it, they prepared to make war, and battled furiously [against the Britons]. And multitudes were slain on either side, but at the last Constantine and the Britons won the day through the slaughter of their enemies.

And when this was done, they came to Silchester,[346] where Constantine ascended the throne.

And for his wife was given to him the daughter of one of the nobility of Rome, who had lived under the protection of Guithelinus the archbishop. And by her, he, Constantine, had three sons, to wit Constans, Ambrosius and Uther,

---

341) The Romans pulled out of Britain in ca AD 429, although Rome's responsibility for Britain's defence was not officially repudiated until AD 446 (see note 343).
342) LXI = *Gittiws*. GoM (6:3) = *Agicius*. Gildas = *Agitium* (see note 343). This is Aetius Flavius (AD 390-454), who was famed for defeating Attila the Hun in 451. He was eventually stabbed to death by Valentinian II.
343) Gildas (chap. 20) gives the following details: "So the miserable remnants sent off a letter again, this time to the Roman commander Aetius, in the following terms -'To Aetius, thrice consul: the groans of the British....The barbarians push us back to the sea, the sea pushes us back to the barbarians; between these two kinds of death, we are either drowned or slaughtered.' But they got no help in return." (Morris, pp. 234).
344) As in GoM (6:4). LXI = *Aldwr*.
345) As in GoM (6:5). LXI = *Kystennin*.
346) LXI = *kaer vyddav*.

[he who was to become] the Pendragon.[347] And Constans had been raised in the monastery of St Amphibalus at Winchester,[348] whilst the others had been raised by Guithelinus. And after Constantine had reigned peacefully for twelve years,[349] there came [to him] a certain Pict, who, under pretext of speaking with him alone and privily, plunged a knife into the top of his breast. And he, Constantine, died of that wound.

And when Constantine was dead, there arose a great dispute amongst the nobles of the realm concerning the election of a new king. Some wished to have Ambrosius for their king, but others were swayed towards Uther, whilst yet others wished to make one of their own friends the king. But at the last, when no agreement could be reached between them, there came Vortigern[350] before them. And he was one of the elders of the land of Britain whose wisdom was deemed the highest. And having judged [before the council] that but one of the sons of Constantine was rightful heir to the crown, he went to Winchester and asked Constans the Monk,[351] for he was the eldest of Constantine's sons, what reward he would give him if he made him the king. And the monk avowed that he would bestow upon him all that he desired in return. And so Vortigern, disdaining the abbot's protests and those of the brothers, led the youth away from the monastery and anointed him king.

And at the passing of some years, Vortigern treasonably considered how he might himself be made king. And so he told the king that many ships were upon the seas but that none could tell where they might land, and that it would be wise to fortify the castles with men, weapons and provisions. And the king commanded him to do all according to his will, for he had conferred upon him the governance of the realm. And when Vortigern had received the king's reply, he visited in person every castle. And he selected eighty[352] sons from amongst the noblest families of the Picts to wait upon the king [during the royal progress] at the head of his stallion. And as time went by, Vortigern kept them content with honours and bribes and comfortable duties.

And upon a certain night in the king's hall, as they were drinking wine whilst he, the king, slept, Vortigern lamented to the Picts that, having little wealth, he could be but of small service to them. "Were it in my power to

---

347) LXI = *Konstant, Emrys,* and *Ythyr ben dragwn,* respectively.
348) LXI = *kaer Wynt.* GoM (8:9) = *Mount Ambrius* (LXI = *Amffibalys*), which is better known today as Amesbury in Wiltshire.
349) GoM (6:5) states ten years.
350) As in GoM (6:6). LXI = *Gwrtheyrn Gwrthenav.*
351) LXI = *Konstant Vynarch* - '*vynarch*' being the radical form of *mynarch* - monk.
352) GoM (6:7) states a hundred Pictish soldiers.

honour any, I would honour you," [he said]. "But surely it is you who rule here?" they cried. "No," [said he], "I tell you truly, I have no estate save Erging and Eyas." And then, Vortigern having fallen asleep, they stole into the king's bedchamber, cut off his head, and came again to Vortigern, throwing the head in his lap and saying, "Have this, and be king if you will."

And when Vortigern saw the head, he wept - through duplicity rather than wrath - and he commanded that the men be arrested and cast into prison.[353] And when the nobility of Britain had heard of the slaying of their king, they assembled in London, commanded that the eighty who had slain the king be hanged, and entrusted the rule of the kingdom to Vortigern until a lawful king could be found. And when Guithelinus had learned of the king's death, he fled in secret to Gurgant,[354] the earl of Kent, and his fleeing was unknown to any of the nobility. But when the princes and nobles learned of it, they were grieved at heart, as were the sons [of Vortigern] with them, whose names were Katigern, Vortimer and Paschent.[355]

And in those days did the bishop Germanus and his companion Lupus[356] preach in the land anew the Gospel of Christ, for since the coming of the pagans there had been seeds of doubt sown amongst the faithful through the false teachings of that arch-heretic Pelagius.[357] For that man had poisoned the faith of the Britons. But through the teachings of these holy men, were the Britons restored to the faith of the catholic church.[358]

And then came Hengist[359] before the king, and desired him to dine with him. And of all the women on earth, the daughter of Hengist, Rowena, was amongst the fairest. And the king desired that he might bed with her that night, and he did so by promising to wed her. And the following day said Hengist to the king, "This day you are my son and I am your father. And it is good therefore that you should heed my counsel alone from this day forth. And I shall counsel you well so that you shall not be dispossessed by the foreign invader. Summon my son

---

353) An authentic flavour of the times is seen in the fact that there was apparently some uncertainty as to whether Vortigern was guilty of the king's death. GoM (6:8) complains that it was never resolved.
354) LXI = *Gwrgant*, who is not mentioned in GoM.
355) As in GoM (6:12). LXI = *Kyndayrn*, *Gwerthevyr*, and *Passgen*, respectively.
356) St Germanus of Auxerre and Lupus of Troyes. LXI = *Simawn* and *Lippys*. Their visit to Britain to extirpate the heresy took place in AD 429.
357) LXI = *Pelagian*.
358) The universal (catholic) Christian faith at this time rather than the Roman Catholic faith.
359) As in GoM (6:11). LXI = *Hainssiestr*.

Octa from Germany, with his uncle Asaf,[360] a great and famous warrior, and give them that land of Scotland which wars against you continually. And they shall defend it from the foreign invader."

Whereupon the king did send into Germany and summon those men, and there arrived from Germany three hundred longships filled with warriors, with Octa and Asaf and Cerdic[361] to lead them into the land of Britain. And when the nobility of the land had learned of it, they were dismayed at the multitude that was reported to have come ashore. And they demanded of the king that he should expel them and drive them away. But upon hearing them, Vortigern did nothing but embolden the men of Germany by granting them lands and riches.

And on seeing this, the Britons chose Vortimer,[362] the son of Vortigern, for their king. And they began to wage war upon the Saxons. And Vortimer won four battles against them, to wit the battle beside the river Avon,[363] the second battle at Aylesford[364] where Katigern and Horsa fought together, each slaying the other.[365] And the third battle was on the seashore from whence the Saxons retreated to the Isle of Thanet,[366] with Vortimer slaughtering them as they fled. And when the Saxons saw that there was no place further to which they might flee, they abandoned their womenfolk and their children and fled the country. And when Vortimer had defeated them [in a fourth battle], he returned to the island of Britain.

And when Rowena, the wife of Vortigern, saw that the Saxons had all been killed, she gave gold and silver to his, Vortimer's, own servant that he might poison the king [Vortimer]. And when he, Vortimer, perceived that he had been poisoned, he called together the nobility and exhorted them every one to protect their land against the [Saxon] tribes, faithful to their most solemn vows. And he apportioned his wealth amongst all his princes, and commanded them to burn his body. And his ashes [he commanded] to be placed inside the bronze likeness of a man. And the likeness must be displayed in any place where the Saxons

---

360) LXI = *Octa* and *Assaf*. GoM (6:13) = *Octa* and *Ebissa*.
361) LXI = *Kledric*. GoM (6:13) = *Cherdic*.
362) LXI = *Gwerthevyr* (see note 355).
363) GoM (6:13) agrees with Nennius (chap. 44) in placing this battle at the river Derwent. The original Welsh reads, "*ar dervyn Avon*," which can mean on the river Dervyn (Derwent).
364) Thought by some to be Fishford. However, GoM (6:13) states Epiford, as does Nennius who also gives its correct British name, *Rhyd yr afael*. The Welsh chronicle's *ryd y pissgod* is evidently the misreading of a damaged text. Today the place is known as Aylesford in Kent.
365) Katigern's tomb is marked today by the famous Kit's [Katigern's] Coty stones near Aylesford.
366) LXI = *ynys Daned*.

might land, for they would surely not land where they saw his likeness [awaiting them]. But when Vortimer was dead, the nobles did not do according to his will, but buried his body in London.[367] And they elected Vortigern to rule over them the second time for want of a rightful king.

And after he, Vortigern, had regained the crown a second time, Rowena sent to her father in Germany, telling him that Vortimer was dead and beseeching him to raise a mighty army and to come [again] to the land of Britain. And on hearing [of the death of Vortimer], Hengist arrived [on the shores of Britain] with sixty longships filled with armed warriors.[368] And when the Britons had learned of the arrival of such a host, they entreated the king to drive them back. But when the Saxons knew of it, they protested to the king and to his nobles that they had come to this land bearing no enmity whatever towards the Britons. "But," [said they], "supposing that the mighty Vortimer was not dead, we brought this host with us lest he should war against us. But on seeing that he is dead, we beseech the king to appoint a day and a place where we may learn his will concerning how many of us may remain here. And however many may not remain, those same shall return to our own land."

And the day that was set was [Beltain], the first of May, [and the place was] the great plain of Kymry. And it was ordained that none should bring weapons to the congress, lest discord should erupt between the delegates. But Hengist, intending to employ his habit of duplicity, commanded each of his men to attend the appointed place with a long dagger [concealed] in his leggings, and that when he sent up the cry, "Draw your knives!", then they should slay the Britons before they could know of it.

And on the appointed day, the king and his nobles came to the place, and the Saxons stood opposite to them. And as the congress stood together in a crowd in conference with one another, so Hengist cried aloud, "Draw your knives!"[369] And the Saxons took out their knives and slew four hundred and sixty[370] of the Britons, including earls, barons and knights. And the king himself was held fast by Hengist. And of all the nobility of Britain, there was none escaped save Eldol,[371] earl of Gloucester, who broke loose with the aid of a cudgel which he saw on the ground. And with that cudgel, he slew seventy men.

---

367) Nennius (chap. 44) says Vortimer was buried in Lincoln -*In Lincolnia enim sepultus est*. However, London is the more likely place.
368) GoM (6:15) states that Hengist came with an unlikely three hundred thousand men.
369) Nennius records the command as, "*Eu, nimet saxas!*"
370) GoM (6:15) agrees with this figure, although Nennius (chap. 46) states that three hundred only of the British nobility were slain.
371) As in GoM (6:16). LXI = *Eidiol*.

And so he came away unscathed and returned to his own estates.

And the Saxons wrested from the king's possession the cities of London, Eboracum and Lincoln.[372] And then the king was set free, but was banished the realm of Lloegria throughout its borders. And so he fled to Kymry. And when it had been so with him for some time, he determined to build a castle lest the Saxons should do to him as they had done before. And having ranged throughout the land of Kymry in his search for a place to build, he came upon a mound well fitted for a castle that is called to this day the Hill of Ambrosius, [which is] in Snowdonia.[373]

And when he gathered there many stonemasons, he began the building of the walls. But all that was built in the day, crumbled and fell in the night. And when this had been the case for some time, with the work not advancing, Vortigern was astonished, and he asked the twelve chief druids what he should do that the building might prosper. And they conferred as to what answer they should give. And then one of their number, [knowing that their safety lay in setting the king an impossible task], said, "Let us [tell the king that he must search] for something which cannot be found, and do a deed that can never be done. And so [the fault of it shall be his, whilst] we shall escape condemnation."

So then they said to the king that if the blood of a boy who was conceived without a father could be found, and mixed with the mortar,[374] then would the building prosper. And when they told this to the king, then sent he throughout the land to find a boy with no father. And when all the land had been searched, then came they to the town of Carmarthen,[375] so named from the legion of ten thousand who were once encamped there. And they saw there some boys playing ball, and two of them began to squabble. "Hold your tongue," said the one to the other, "and do not liken yourself to me. For I was born of gentle parentage, but for your birth there was no father!"

And upon hearing these words, the messengers laid hold on the lad and brought him to the chief councillor of the town, and commanded him in the name of the king to present the lad and his mother before the king. And that he did, and the king demanded of the woman who the child's

---

372) LXI = *Kaer Lyndain, Kaer Efroc* and *Kaer Lincol,* respectively. GoM (6:16) has York, Lincoln and Winchester.
373) LXI = *Yrri,* i.e. Snowdonia (mod. Welsh *Eryri*). The hill concerned still carries its ancient name of *dinas Emreis.*
374) The mingling of blood and mortar was a distinctly Celtic pagan ritual.
375) LXI = *kaer Vyrddin.*

father was. "Upon mine oath, I know not," she said. "I am the only daughter of the king of Dyfed, and whilst I was yet a damsel I was made a nun at Carmarthen. And as I slept amongst my sisters, there came, whilst I slept, a young man who lay with me. But on waking, there was none save my sisters and myself. And after these things, I conceived and bare this son. Upon my faith in God, no more than this has ever happened betwixt myself and any man."

And the king demanded of bishop Maygan,[376] "Can this thing be true?" "Why, yes," said he, "for when Lucifer and the angels who shared in his sin fell with him, then wherever they were at the time when God overthrew them, and in whatever guise they chanced to be, then that is their state to this present day. And some have the power to take on a woman's shape, and some a man's. And this, perchance, is how the lad was conceived."[377]

And so the king told the boy that he must mix his blood with the mortar, that the building might prosper. "But why?" asked the lad. "How is my blood to be preferred above that of any other?"

"Because [that is] the counsel of my twelve chief druids," answered the king.

"Then," said the boy, "summon your twelve druids to this place." And when they had come, the lad demanded of them, "Why told you the king that my blood would cause the building to prosper?" [And when they did not answer, he asked], "What lies beneath those rushes yonder?"

"In truth, we know not," they replied. And the lad commanded that the rushes be dug up, and beneath them there lay a large pool of water. "And what lies within that pool?" the lad asked them. "We cannot tell," replied the druids. "Then," [commanded the boy], "drain the pool, and you shall find therein a stone chest. And within that chest are two dragons. Now they are slumbering, but when they awake they fight, and it is that upheaval that causes the building to fail."

And when they could not draw off the water, Merlin, through his wisdom, drained it away in five channels. Now, hitherto the lad had been known as The Nun's Child.[378] But he was called Merlin from this day on, because he was found in the City of Merlin.[379] And when Vortigern perceived that the boy

---

376) As in LXI. GoM (6:18) = *Maugantius*.
377) GoM (6:18) enlarges considerably on this.
378) LXI = *Annvab y llaian*.
379) At this point, GoM (7:1-4) inserts the *Prophecies of Merlin*. This was never part of the original source material, as GoM himself acknowledges - hence its absence in LXI.

possessed great wisdom, he demanded of him,[380] "And what is to become of me?" And Merlin told him, "You are to perish in the flames, for this very day are the sons of Constantine upon the sea, and tomorrow shall they come ashore at Totnes in Lloegria. And wherever you may be, you must beware of the two sons of Constantine."

And at that, Vortigern commanded the stone chest to be opened. And from it did fly the two dragons, the one white and the other red, and they began to fight ferociously. And straightway the white dragon drove the red into the middle of the pool. But then the red, though stricken, drove back the white, again to the middle of the pool. And Vortigern asked Merlin the meaning of this thing. And Merlin prophesied, "Alas for the red dragon! She hastens to her doom, for the white shall rob her of her domains. [And know that] the white dragon stands for the Saxons, and the red which is to be overcome by the white, stands for the Britons. And because of it shall the mountains become as the valleys, and down the valleys shall blood-laden rivers flow."

And with that, Vortigern asked Merlin [a second time] what kind of death he should suffer.

And he, Merlin, replied, "Beware of the two sons of Constantine, for even now they spread their sails upon the sea of Armorica to come to Britain to free their land from the Saxons. But first shall they burn you in a tower of stone, for by treachery and murder did you betray [both] their father and their brother. And you did beckon the Saxon to come into this land for the sake of your kingly crown. [But know that] this has spelled your doom, for two shameful fates await you, for there is also the Saxon [himself] who overwhelms you. But tomorrow shall come Ambrosius and Uther, the sons of Constantine, with twelve thousand mounted knights. And they shall bespatter the faces of the Saxons with their own blood. And when Hengist is slain, then shall Ambrosius be anointed king. And he shall rule the land and rebuild the churches. But at last through poison shall he die. And after him shall Uther, his brother, be made king, and he also shall die through poison by the traiterous hand of a Saxon. But the Cornish Boar shall wreak vengeance for all these things."

And the very next day did the sons of Constantine set foot in the land of Lloegria. And when news of their coming was spread abroad, all the Britons gathered together to pay fealty to Ambrosius. And he put on the crown and was anointed their king. And then Ambrosius and his council debated awhile whether first he should come against Vortigern or the Saxons. And there was he

---

380) GoM begins Book 8 of *Historia Regum Britanniae* at this point.

urged to come first to Kymry and lay siege to the Castle of Gronwyr,[381] for to that place had Vortigern fled. The same was in Erging on the banks of the Wye.[382] And Ambrosius arrived there with a mighty army and, recalling the crimes committed by Vortigern, he addressed his nobles with these words, "My lords, this man murdered my father and my brother. And treacherously did he beckon the heathen Saxon into this land. Let us therefore bravely assault [him within his] castle yonder." And straightway they laid fires around the castle and put to the flame whatever men or chattels were within - and Vortigern with them.

And Hengist was afraid, for it had been told him that none in the land of Gaul could oppose Ambrosius and live. Notwithstanding he was [also] wise, generous and merciful. And the Saxons therefore fled to the other side of the Humber, and there they did establish themselves to the end that they might dwell there. And when Ambrosius knew of it, he pursued them with his host. And it displeased him sore to see the churches ruined by the Saxons, and he swore that if he returned alive he would restore them all as they had been at their best.

And when Hengist knew that Ambrosius was pursuing him, he belaboured his men to fight manfully, and he told them that Ambrosius commanded but a miserable contingent of the horsemen of Gaul - whereas they had no need to fear the Britons when they, the Saxons, were forty thousand warriors. And then they came to a place called Maes Beli,[383] and [there] they planned to make a sudden and unexpected assault upon Ambrosius and his army. But Ambrosius foresaw it and gathered his host to him, and intermingled his own soldiers with those of Gaul. And he stationed the men of Dyfed upon the hills to his flank, and the men of Gwynedd in a copse close by, that they might engage the Saxons no matter the direction from which they might come.

And as for the enemy, Hengist addressed and encouraged his men, and when many had fallen on either side, Hengist and all his host took flight to a place called Conisborough.[384] And Ambrosius and his men pursued them there, as it has been told [elsewhere], and slew them. But many escaped to a castle close at hand where they regrouped a second time and fought desperately on every side. But at last the men of Ambrosius, thanks to the skill of their leaders, broke through and scattered the Saxon host. And Eidol, the earl of Gloucester,

---

381) As in LXI. GoM (8:2) = *Genoreu*. GoM states that the castle stood on the hill of *Cloartius*, which is known today as Little Doward in Monmouthshire.
382) LXI = *Gwy*.
383) As in LXI. GoM (8:4) = *Maisbeli*.
384) LXI = *kaer Kynan*. GoM (8:5) = *Cunungeburg*.

sought for Hengist and found him at last. And wildly did they fight, and fire flashed from their swords like lightning when it thunders. And behold, at this time came Gorlois,[385] the earl [of Cornwall], with his men, and dispersed the Saxon host. And so, spurred on by an angry will, Eidol took Hengist by the beard and helmet, and hauling him through the midst of his own men, cried out with all his might, "Now exterminate the Saxons, for they are defeated. Behold now, here is Hengist!"

And at that, the Saxons took flight. And Octa, the son of Hengist, fled with his host to Eboracum. And Asaf, his uncle, with what remained of his army, fled to Alclud. And having won the day, Ambrosius came to Conisborough aforementioned, and captured the castle. And there he remained for three days to bury the dead, heal the wounded and refresh his men. And Ambrosius sought counsel concerning Hengist, and in the council were the bishop of Gloucester and his brother the earl, to wit Eidol. And when the bishop saw Hengist standing before him, he cried, "My lords, should each of you elect to set Hengist free, then I would slay him myself. For so did Samuel the Prophet when he saw Agag, the king of the Amalekites, in chains. And he, Samuel, said to him, 'Forasmuch as you have deprived mothers of their sons, so shall I make your mother sonless!' - and he cut him in pieces!"[386] And Eidol took Hengist to the top of a hill close to the castle, and he cut off his head. And he cried a mournful wail over the head, as is the manner when burying a warrior.[387]

And Ambrosius went from that place to Eboracum to seek Octa. And Octa was advised by his counsellors to yield himself and his people to Ambrosius, standing before him with each man holding a chain [to signify his captivity], and with ashes upon the head of every man [to signify their repentance], and say to him, "O mighty king, our gods are vanquished, and we know of a truth that your God, Who has delivered into your hand in this manner so many mighty men as these, is all powerful. And here we present ourselves, lord, subject to your will, and each with a chain in his hand [as a token thereof], ready even to be put to death if it be your pleasure."

And Ambrosius sought counsel from the bishop and Eidol, who said, "You wicked men have come here, freely to seek mercy [at our hands], even as the heathen came to Israel. And they received the mercy [they begged for]. Even

---

385) As in GoM (8:6). LXI = *Gwrlais*.
386) The bishop is referring to the story of the slaying of Agag, king of the Amalekites, by the prophet Samuel (1 Sam. 15:32-3).
387) LXI = *ssawden*, a word already obsolete by the 12th century. It means a warrior, and what is described here is the ancient Celtic ritual of taking off a prisoner's head and honouring it.

so, our mercy shall be nothing less than Israel's."[388]

And so Octa and his people were shewn mercy by Ambrosius, and they were granted land where they might serve him in perpetual servitude, which land was Scotland. And so peace was wrought between them. And so came Ambrosius to Eboracum where he summoned all his earls, his barons and his archbishops. And it was proclaimed by that council that all the churches that had been destroyed by the Saxons, would be rebuilt at the king's own charges. And after fifteen days, he came to London where also he commanded that all churches be restored, all bad laws amended, all lands wrongfully appropriated to be restored to their rightful owners, and justice to be given to all who might seek it. And from here came he to Winchester to do likewise.

And having pacified all his realm, he went to Salisbury[389] to inspect the graves of those whom Hengist had treacherously slain there, earls, barons and others of nobility. And there were three hundred monks who lived in the monastery of Mount Ambrius, which same monastery had been so named from its founder, Ambri. And Ambrosius was grieved to see the place in ruins. And he summoned all the stonemasons and carpenters in the land to build a permanent monastery, beautifully adorned, around those hallowed tombs. But when the craftsmen had gathered there together, and could not proceed with the work, then Tamor,[390] archbishop of Caerleon-on-Usk, approached Ambrosius and said to him, "Call Merlin to your side, my liege, the druid of Vortigern, for he has unheard of knowledge and strange gifts indeed by which he is able to overcome such things."

And so was Merlin brought before Ambrosius, and the king rejoiced to see him.[391] But upon Ambrosius asking him for prophecies that he might learn what may befall his kingdom, Merlin answered him, "Such prognostications are unlawful save when necessity compels them. And if I were to speak of such things without necessity, then the Spirit who guides me would leave me in my hour of need."

And at that was the king mindful to enquire no more of him, save asking how he would devise the building of a beautiful and everlasting memorial in that place. And Merlin counselled him to set out for Ireland, to the Giant's Ring

---

388) LXI = *iddewon*, lit. the Jews.
389) LXI = *ssaltsbri*, a phonetic rendering of the Saxon name for that city. It was originally known to the Britons as *Kaer Graddawc*, which GoM variously renders *Kaercaradduc* (8:9) and *Ridcaradoch* (8:19): "...which is now called Salisbury."
390) As in LXI. GoM (8:10) = *Tremorinus*.
391) According to GoM (8:10), Merlin was found by the Galabes Springs, known in the Book of Llandaff as *Nant i Galles*, in the land of the Gewissei. This was *Gwenhwys*, or the land of the men of Gwent.

on Mount Killara[392] - "For there are stones in that place whose nature is mysterious and of which no man knows anything. And not by might nor by power, but by wisdom only can they be brought here. But once they are here, they shall stand for all time."

But Ambrosius laughed, and said, "And how might they be fetched from that place?" And Merlin replied, "Laugh not, my lord, for I tell you but what is true. They are indeed stones of mysterious power within which are properties of healing. And in ancient times did giants fetch them to where they stand this day, from the farthest reaches of Spain.[393] And they fetched them for this purpose. When one of their number fell sick, they would make a balm in the midst of the stones. Then, washing the stones with water, they mixed the water with the balm and were healed of their wounds by it. And they put herbs in the balm which [herbs] also healed their wounds."

And on learning of these things, the king straightway set out to retrieve the stones. And he sent Uther Pendragon commanding fifteen thousands warriors, and Merlin with him also, for he was the wisest amongst all those of his generation. And in those days did Gillomaur[394] rule in Ireland. And he came to them with a mighty army, and enquired of them the nature of their mission. And when the king learned the reason for their coming, he mocked them and cried, "It is little to be wondered at that any weak nation can lay waste the land of Britain, when the Britons are so feebleminded that they declare war on the people of Ireland over some stones!"

And on joining battle, they fought desperately while many fell on either side - until Gillomaur took flight and abandoned his men. And then said Merlin, "Use any means you can to remove the stones." But they could not do so. And Merlin laughed [at their efforts], and with wisdom and but little labour did he remove the stones to the ships. And so were they brought to Mount Ambri. And to that place did Ambrosius summon all his earls and his barons, and all the sacred scholars of the realm, to seek their counsel how he might beautify the place and adorn it. And Ambrosius wore upon his head the crown of the kingdom, and with worship did celebrate Whitsun for three days. And he bestowed upon his subjects their lawful rights, and enriched his noblemen with gold and silver, steeds and arms, as befitted each of them. And having all things

---

392) As in LXI. GoM (8:19) = *Mount Killarus*. GoM greatly enlarges on the following conversation. Stonehenge is still known to the modern Welsh as *Cor y Cewri*, the Giant's Ring.
393) LXI = *Yssbaen*. GoM (8:11) states that the stones were brought to Ireland from the remotest regions of Africa.
394) LXI = *Gilamwri*. GoM (8:12) = *Gillomanius*.

prepared, Ambrosius commanded Merlin to assemble the stones as they had been at Killara. And this he did, and all acknowledged that wisdom is better than strength.

And in those days Paschent, a son of Vortigern, had escaped to Germany where he mustered an army, the greatest he could find, by promising them all manner of riches should they come with him and win back the land of Britain from Ambrosius, son of Constantine. And they believed Paschent and came with him, and a host of armed warriors also. And when the ships came to this land, they began to lay waste the country. And hearing of it, Ambrosius met them with a mighty army and drove them headlong into Ireland where Gillomaur [still] ruled as king. And he, Gillomaur, behaved amicably towards Paschent, and together they grumbled about the sons of Constantine. And then, by a mutual compact, they came together with a fleet to Menevia.[395]

And when Uther heard of it, he was greatly troubled, for Ambrosius lay sick at Winchester, whilst he himself had not might enough to meet Paschent and Gillomaur in open battle. And they, Paschent and Gillomaur, when they both knew of it, were pleased that Ambrosius lay sick, thinking that Uther could not come against them both alone. And then came a certain Saxon to Paschent [who was] named Eppa,[396] and he asked him what reward he would give to the man who should kill Ambrosius. "A thousand pounds would I give to that man and count him my friend to the end of my days should I be king," Paschent replied, "and I would heap lands upon him and riches to his heart's content."

To which Eppa answered, "I know of an antidote against Ambrosius as well as the manner [and tongue] of the Britons. Give me but a pledge of all you have promised, and I shall bring about the death of Ambrosius."

And [so] they made a compact. And Eppa shaved his head and his beard after the manner of a monk, and took the implements of a physician with him to the court of Ambrosius. And he caused himself to be made known to some in the palace, saying that he was an accomplished healer. And being delighted to receive him, they announced his arrival to Ambrosius. Whereupon he, Eppa, concocted a poisonous draught for the king, and he, the king, drank it down.

---

395) LXI = *Myniw*. GoM (8:14) states that they landed near the town of Menevia. LXI's Miniw is simply the radical form of *Kaer Vyniw*, which is the modern St Davids.

396) As in LXI. GoM (8:14) = *Eopa*. Manley Pope adds a gloss to this episode that may help us date more accurately the year of Emrys' death. He states: "In the catalogue of comets given by Shelburne at the end of his Manilius, a comet is described as having appeared AD 454 or 457. Another of AD 504, crowned with a dragon, is more probably the same that is said to have been seen by Uther. Henry of Huntingdon dates the death of Emrys, AD 503 [N.B. I can find no such reference in Henry of Huntingdon]. It is therefore likely, that the comet of AD 504 was the one seen by Uther, and if so, we have the true date of the death of Emrys."

And the betrayer counselled him after to rest privily that the poison might take a more speedy effect. And so Eppa disappeared from the court.

And in those days a star of wondrous size appeared to Uther, having but a single tail. And at the head of the tail glowed the form of a dragon, from whose mouth issued two shafts of light, the one pointing towards the farthest reaches of Gaul, and the other towards Ireland which divided up into seven thinner shafts of light. And Uther and they who saw the star with him were greatly troubled, and they enquired of the druids what it might portend. And Merlin, weeping, said, "O land of the Britons, now are you robbed of the mighty Ambrosius, a loss that cannot be amended. Yet notwithstanding, you do not want for another like him, for you, Uther, shall be king. Hasten to face your enemies and you shall win the whole realm, for it is you who are portended by this star like a shining dragon. And the shaft of light over Gaul portends a son of yours who shall prosper and conquer many lands. And the other shaft of light portends a daughter of yours whose lineage shall have an inheritance forever!"

And Uther, though doubtful of Merlin's words, assaulted his enemies and made war against them, and many fell on either side. But at the last, Uther gained the victory, driving Paschent and Gillomaur headlong to their ships and slaying [their men], as we have already recounted. And having won the day, Uther returned to Winchester to bury Ambrosius, his brother. And to that place came all the archbishops, bishops and abbots in the land. And Ambrosius was buried within the monastery of Ambri, within the Giant's Ring.

And Uther called a council and by common assent was anointed king, and the crown of the realm was placed upon his head. And Uther recalled the words that Merlin had spoken to him, and Uther gave orders for two golden dragons to be made and fashioned with wondrous skill in the likeness of that star that he had seen at the end of the shaft of light. And Uther presented one of these dragons to the church at Winchester, but the other he carried before him into battle, from which moment henceforth he was called Uther the Pendragon.

And when they knew that Ambrosius was dead, then did Octa, the son of Hengist, and Asaf [his uncle], rally the Saxons together. And they said to the Saxons that they were henceforth freed from their oath [of subservience] to Ambrosius. And so they sent to Germany and also to Paschent for help, and having gathered a mighty army they overran all Lloegria as far as Eboracum. And upon their having invested the city, Uther came with his army and there was a great battle. And at the last the Saxons were routed and driven headlong to the mountain called Danned.[397] And that was a great and high mountain, full

---

397) LXI = *mynydd daned*, lit. the Toothed Mountain, *daned* later developing into *danheddog*, the modern Welsh for toothed. GoM (8:18) = *Mount Damen*.

of crags and stones. And there the Saxons rested that night.

And Uther summoned his counsellors before him, and Gorlois, the earl of Cornwall, arose and said, "Our numbers are far fewer than theirs, my lord. Therefore, let us attack them under cover of night, and [so] shall we defeat them with little loss." And so did they, and rushed the mountain, slaying a great number. And they took Octa and Asaf captive and scattered all the rest. And having won the day, Uther went up to Alclud and from there he travelled all around the kingdom, enforcing the rule of law so that no man dared harm another. And having pacified the realm, the king came to London where he put Octa and Asaf into prison. And he celebrated Easter there, and summoned to the feast all the earls and barons in the land, and their wives with them. And Uther entertained them splendidly, and they spent the festival in opulence and rejoicing.

And to that feast came Gorlois, earl of Cornwall, whose wife was Ygerna, daughter to the noble Amlawdd.[398] And there was in all the land of Britain neither dame nor damsel as fair as she. And when Uther saw her, he desired her greatly so that he could not conceal [his great love towards her]. Neither could he live without her, but sent her many love tokens, intoxicants in golden cups, and many silly messages. And the earl Gorlois learned of it and was enraged. And he went away from the court without [first seeking] leave of the king. And when Uther heard of it, he was angry, and sent a herald after Gorlois commanding that he should return to court, for it was a great offence to the king to go from his court without leave. And he sent a second herald, and then a third, but still Gorlois would not come. And so the king proclaimed that he would ruin him by fire and sword if he would not come. But still Gorlois refused for all the threats against him.

And the king quickly mustered an army and ravaged and burned the land throughout Gorlois' estates. And so Gorlois, because he lacked the men to meet the king in open battle, fortified two castles which he possessed, into the strongest of which he put his wife. And that castle was called Tintagel,[399] which was on the sea shore. But he went himself to his other castle [which is] called Dimilioc,[400] lest either castle should fall.

---

398) LXI = *Amlawdd wledic*. The family tree of *Ygerna* (LXI's *Eigr*) is more fully supplied in the story of Culhwch and Olwen. See Appendix I.
399) As in GoM (8:19). LXI = *Tindagol*.
400) As in GoM (8:19). LXI = *Tinblot*. Thorpe (p. 206) tells us: "Near the village of Pendoggett, some 5 1/2 miles south-west of Tintagel, lies a great encampment of three concentric ramparts and ditches, some 448 yards in overall diameter, which bears the name of Tregeare Rounds and is known locally as Castle Dameliock."

And Uther and all his host besieged the castle [Dimilioc] in which Gorlois was [hiding], and put the men [of Gorlois] to flight and almost killed him. And a herald was despatched to tell Ygerna of these things. And then Uther called before him one Ulfin, knight of Salisbury,[401] and he opened to him his heart, telling him of his love for Ygerna and asking him what he should do. And Ulfin said, "My liege, it would be madness to try to force an entry into the castle where Ygerna lies, for it stands upon a crag above the sea, with but a single entrance leading to it. And three knights could hold that entrance against all the world.[402] This is my counsel therefore. Summon Merlin before you and open your heart to him, for if that man is able to help you, he surely will."

And this the king did. And Merlin said, "If this be your desire, then you must take on the likeness of Gorlois whilst I myself assume the likeness of Brithael,[403] his favourite squire. And I will put upon Ulfin the likeness of Medaf of Tintagel,[404] and none shall know that we are not Gorlois and his two squires. And when they had thus been transfigured, they set out and came to the gateway of Tintagel castle by eventide. And they announced to the porter that Gorlois was come. And the porter opened to them and they entered [the castle]. And Uther lay down with Ygerna and by false affection and lying words told her that he had stolen away from the other castle to be with her, and that [such was his love for her that] he could in no wise refrain from seeing her. And she believed [his words], and that night was conceived Arthur, the son of Uther [Pendragon].

And when Uther's men learned that he, Uther, was not with them [at Castle Dimilioc], they assaulted the castle so heavily that Gorlois was compelled to sally forth and do battle against them. And Gorlois was slain and his army scattered. And straightway there came runners to bring tidings to Ygerna concerning these things. But Uther, who was with her in bed and who still wore the likeness of Gorlois, laughed and said, "But lady, I am not slain. But I must go now and see what men I have lost." And then Uther returned to his host in his own guise, and was at once grieved for the death of Gorlois, but pleased also [for the seduction of Ygerna]. And from that day forth, Uther took Ygerna for his secret wife, and had by her a son named Arthur and a daughter named Anna, his sister.

And after many years, Uther was stricken with disease and was sick for a

401) LXI = *Wlffin kaer Gradawc*. GoM (8:19) = *Ulfin of Ridcaradoch* - (see note 389).
402) A very accurate appraisal of the approach to Tintagel Castle.
403) As in LXI. GoM (8:19) = *Britaelis*.
404) As in LXI. GoM (8:19) = *Jordan of Tintagel*.

long time. And he grievously offended the custodians of Octa and Asaf, and in their hatred towards him they released those [Saxon] nobles and let them flee the country. And they went with them to Germany, and when the Britons learned that the Saxons were returning to invade the land, they feared greatly. And their fears were realized, for they, the Saxons, came to Albany and laid waste the land and burned it.

And Loth,[405] the son of Kynvarch [and lord of Lothian], was commander of the hosts of Britain. He it was who married Anna,[406] the daughter of Uther Pendragon. And he was a mighty and a princely man who worshipped truth, and in many wars did he fight against the Saxons though the Saxons oft defeated him. And when it had been so for some years, and he had lost to them almost the entire kingdom, it was told to Uther that the earl had failed to overcome the Saxons. And Uther was angered exceedingly, and summoned all the nobles of the realm before him to reproach them for their faint-heartedness towards the Saxons. And in that council Uther was advised to let himself be carried in a litter before his army to the town of Verulamium, for in that place were the Saxons killing and burning.

And when Octa and Asaf were told that Uther was sick, and that he was coming before his host to that place in a litter, they were glad and mocked him with contempt, and called him a half dead man. And the Saxons left open the gates when they entered the city in contempt of Uther and all his host. And when Uther knew of it, he invested the city and many of his men entered. And there were many slain on either side until nightfall. And in the morning, the Saxons sallied forth out of the city and battled desperately against the Britons. But Octa and Asaf were both slain there, and the rest of the Saxons fled in disgrace. And Uther, in his joy, sat up in his litter, although hitherto he could be turned only by the strength of two men, and he cried, "Those lying traitors said I was a half dead man. But the half dead man who conquers [his foes] is greater than the half alive man who is conquered [by him]. And I would rather die in glory than live in shame!"

And after this victory, the remainder of the Saxons who had fled, met up again in Albany to do battle as before. And Uther wished to pursue them, but his counsellors would not allow it, for he was too feeble to be carried there by litter. And for this cause did the Saxons grow more arrogant, and they determined to kill Uther by stealth. And they sent men disguised as freedmen to

---

405) LXI = Llew. GoM (8:21) = *Loth of Lodonesia.*
406) Anna is said (by GoM) to have later married Budicius II, king of Brittany. GoM's reference is to *Budic of Cornouaille* (Cornwall) in Brittany, who reigned some time before AD 530.

talk with him, and these sent back word that Uther would drink only water from a certain well near Verulamium. So they poisoned this well and the springs close by, so that when Uther drank of the water he died, as did many others who drank after him [until the cause of their deaths was discovered].[407] And the Britons filled in the wells with earth, and they buried Uther in the Giant's Ring.[408]

And the Saxons sent to Germany for help in conquering the land of Britain. And there was raised for them a mighty fleet, with Colgrim[409] to lead them. And they overran [the country] from the Humber to Cape Bladdon. And when the nobility of Britain heard of it, they summoned to Silchester all the laity and clergy in the land because of the Saxon peril. And in council it was decided to anoint Arthur as king, even though he was not old enough to wear the crown, being but fifteen years of age. But there was no man who was known by any there to possess the same genius as he. And Arthur bestowed all that he had, and more. And then the princes of the realm charged Dubricius,[410] archbishop of Caerleon-on-Usk, to anoint Arthur king, and to place upon his head the crown. [And this they did] for fear of the pagan Saxons.

And straightway Arthur assembled a mighty host and marched to Eboracum. And on hearing it, Colgrim mustered a great force of Saxons, Scots and Picts, and bravely engaged Arthur in battle upon the banks of the river Douglas.[411] And many were slain on either side, but in the end Arthur finally won the day and compelled Colgrim to flee. And he, Colgrim, escaped with his host to Eboracum where Arthur laid siege to them to starve them.

And when Baldulf,[412] the brother of Colgrim, heard of it, he came up with a host of six thousand to within ten miles of Eboracum. The same Baldulf had been awaiting the arrival of Cerdic,[413] a prince of Germany, with aid for the Saxon cause. But they, the host of Baldulf, desired to fight Arthur under cover of night. And when Arthur learned of it, he commanded Cador,[414] the earl of Cornwall, to take six hundred mounted warriors and three thousand foot, to halt Baldulf in his path. And when he encountered the Saxon host, Cador waged a

---

407) GoM (8:24) states that a hundred men also died with Uther.
408) Stonehenge. GoM (8:24) states that Uther was buried beside his brother Ambrosius.
409) LXI = *Kolgrin*. GoM (9:1) = *Colgrin*.
410) As in GoM (9:1). LXI = *dyfric*.
411) As in GoM (9:1). LXI = *Dylas*.
412) As in GoM (9:1). LXI = *Baldwlff*.
413) LXI = *Kledric*. GoM (9:1) = *Cheldric*.
414) As in GoM (9:1). LXI = *kattwr*.

mighty battle, and in his rage and violence scattered them, slaying a great many and putting the rest to flight.

And Baldulf, ashamed that he had failed to rescue his brother, deliberated what he should do next. And then he commanded his hair to be cut and his beard to be shaved, and, dressed in the clothes of a minstrel, he wandered through the camp of the Britons until he stood beneath the city wall. And there he sang and recited in a loud voice until [he was] answered from within the city. And they pulled him up with ropes over the wall, and he and his brother deliberated how they might break out from that place. And whilst they were so deliberating, behold, the heralds arrived [to say that help had come] from Germany with six hundred longships filled with warriors, with Cerdic commanding them. And they came ashore in Albany.

And on hearing of it, Arthur left Eboracum and went to London, and summoned his princes before him to take counsel of them. And their counsel was to send to Howel,[415] the son of Ambrosius of Armorica, Arthur's sister's son who was king of Armorica,[416] to seek his help. And Howel came with fifteen thousand warriors to Southampton[417] in the land of Lloegria. And Arthur rejoiced to see him, and from thence they journeyed together to Kaer Lwyttgoed, which is Lincoln, for the Saxons were in that place. And a mighty battle was waged there in which six thousand Saxons perished from both slaughter and drowning. And those who survived took flight to the Caledonian Forest where Arthur pursued them.

And a mighty battle followed in which multitudes were slain on either side, for the Britons were hindered [from slaughtering the Saxons] because the oak woods [sheltered the Saxons from them]. And so Arthur commanded that the oaks be cut down and built into a mighty stockade around the Saxons [to hem them in]. And for three days and nights they starved the Saxon host. And then, that they might not die of hunger, the Saxons yielded up to Arthur all their spoil, and tribute also from Germany, that they might return unmolested to their own land. And for this were hostages given. But once upon the sea, they repented of their undertakings to Arthur and turned about, coming ashore at Totnes in Lloegria.

And they pillaged the land as far as the Severn, and from there went to

---

415) As in LXI. GoM (9:2) = *Hoel*, who reigned as king ca AD 510-45.
416) Curiously, GoM (9:2) names Howel's father as *Budicius*.
417) LXI = *Northamtwn*, which is clearly a misreading of *Porth Hamwnt*, Southampton. GoM (9:2) correctly identifies the place. See also note 480.

Silchester[418] where they invested and besieged the city. And when Arthur knew of it, he straightway hanged the hostages. And he left off fighting the Scots and the Picts, leaving Howel, his nephew, enfeebled through sickness at Alclud in the midst of his foes. And coming upon the Saxons at Silchester, he said to them, "You traiterous knaves! Because you have not kept faith with me, so neither will I keep faith with you!" And then came Dubricius, archbishop of Caerleon-on-Usk, to a high hill from whence he cried with a loud voice, "My lords, and such as be of Christian faith, remember your kindred this day and avenge their blood upon the Saxons, for by God's help your achievements this day - and your deaths! - will cleanse you from the sin of battle!"

And Arthur put on a royal breast-plate, and upon his head he wore a golden helmet with an image of a dragon upon it, and another image also called Prydwen.[419] And on the inner surface was a carved image of Mary, which Arthur carried with him [to save him from the] danger of battle. And he took up his sword called Excalibur,[420] the finest sword in all the land of Britain [and] which was made in the Isle of Avalon.[421] And in his hand he carried a spear called the Rod of Compelling.[422]

And when all had donned their armour, with the archbishop's blessing they fell furiously upon the enemy, slaying them until nightfall. And as eventide fell, the Saxon host rallied at the top of a high hill where they thought themselves safe. But when the morning came, Arthur took the hill, notwithstanding the Saxons fought with fury. And so in anger did Arthur draw Excalibur, his sword, and calling upon the name of Mary bravely fell upon his enemies, whom he slew with a single stroke. Nor did Arthur cease from killing until he had put to the slaughter four hundred and seventy of the Saxon host.

And when the Britons beheld their king excelling [all others] in deed of war and courage, they exhorted one another to do likewise. And at last, Colgrim and Baldulf, his brother, were slain and many thousands with them. And Cerdic had taken flight, deserting his own men, and Arthur commanded Cador, earl of Cornwall, to pursue him with ten thousand warriors.[423] But Arthur marched back to Alclud where he had heard that the Scots and the Picts were about to dispossess Howel of the city.

---

418) LXI = *kaer Vyddav*. GoM (9:3) has Bath, but here he evidently misreads *Kaer Vaddon* for *Kaer Vyddav*, suggesting a damaged text in the original.
419) As in LXI. *Prydwenn* means an image that is sacred or blessed.
420) LXI = *kaledvwlch*. GoM (9:4) = *Caliburn*.
421) LXI = *ynys afallach*, lit. the Island of Apples.
422) LXI = *Rongymyniad*. GoM (9:4) = *Ron*.
423) GoM doesn't give the size of Cador's army.

In the meantime, Cador and his host commandeered the Saxons' ships, which he filled with his own men, chasing after the remnant like a forest lion. And then was Cerdic, their commander, slain and the survivors reduced to perpetual servitude. And Cador, having routed the Saxon host, went to Alclud where Arthur was, and who had driven the Picts back into the sea. This was the third time that Arthur and Howel had done this.

And then they, the Scots, fled to Loch Lomond,[424] into which loch there flow three hundred and sixty rivers[425] which cascade down the mountains of Prydyn, from whence as a single river they flow towards the sea. And that river is the Leven.[426] And upon each island [in the loch] there is a crag, and upon each crag the nest of an eagle. And when all the eagles fly to the top of a single crag and shriek, then men know that some calamity from abroad will befall the land. And Arthur sailed around the loch in ships and boats, taking prisoner all [the Scots]. And thousands died of hunger. And behold, Gillomaur,[427] the king of Ireland, landed with a mighty fleet to help the Scots, for they were of the same race and language. And on seeing this, Arthur left off [rounding up] the Scots, and did battle with the Irish,[428] and he drove them headlong back to Ireland. And Arthur returned to the Scots a second time to continue as before.

And the bishops and holy abbots stood before Arthur in their robes, and besought him on their knees to spare those people. And those who had survived were to live in perpetual servitude to him and to those who should reign after him. And Arthur consented to this thing, and when peace was settled Howel went to see the loch and its surroundings. And Arthur said to Howel, "Not far away is a lake more wonderful than this. It is twenty feet wide, twenty feet long and five feet deep. And it has four sorts of fish, one sort in each corner, and never do any of the different sorts mingle with the others. And there is another lake near the Severn called Llyn Llion,[429] into which no matter how much fresh water flows, it never fills up to its banks. And at the time of high tide, its own waters ebb! And when the tide ebbs, it fills, throwing up mountainous waves! And if a man faces towards those waves, he will barely escape with his life. But if he turns his back towards them, then he will escape, however close to them he might be."

---

424) LXI = *llimonwy*.
425) GoM (9:6) has sixty streams.
426) LXI = *llefn*. GoM doesn't name the stream.
427) LXI = *Gilamwri*. GoM (9:6) = *Gilmaurius*.
428) LXI = *gwyddyl*, i.e. Goidels or Gaels.
429) LXI = *llyn lliawn*. GoM (9:7) = *Lin Ligua*. Nennius (chap. 69) = *Llyn Lliwan*.

And from that place Arthur went to Eboracum to hold his Christmas court. And Arthur was grieved to see in that place churches destroyed and scholars [who had been] put to death. And Arthur bestowed the land of Scotland upon Aron,[430] a son of Kynvarch. And upon Loth,[431] [another] son of Kynvarch, the earldom of Lindsey. The same was brother-in-law to Arthur, and also to Gwyar,[432] mother of Gawain,[433] the emperor. And upon Urien,[434] a son of Kynvarch, he bestowed Moray.[435] And Arthur pacified the kingdom more effectively than had ever been done [before]. And Arthur took Guinevere[436] to wife, the daughter of the mighty Gogvran.[437] And her mother was of the Roman nobility. And Cador, earl of Cornwall, had raised her, and there was not a fairer than she in all the land of Britain.

And Arthur prepared a fleet to go to Ireland the summer following. And when Arthur landed in that place, Gillomaur with all his host was ready to give battle. But it availed him nothing, for [again] he took flight. And whilst he fled, he was taken [captive] and was compelled to pay fealty to Arthur, both he and all his host. And from thence did Arthur go to Islay[438] and subdue it. And when news of this was heard by many of the other islands -as well as Arthur's prowess in battle, how none could withstand him -then Doldaf,[439] the king of the Scots, and Gwynnwas,[440] the king of the Orkneys, of their own volition paid homage to Arthur, and paid him tribute [also] by the year.

And as winter closed [in], so Arthur returned to the land of Britain, and for twelve years he rested [from his wars] and summoned great and wise men from every land to increase their numbers here. And then went abroad his fame for

---

430) As in LXI. GoM (9:9) = *Auguselus*.
431) As in GoM (9:9). LXI = *Elw*.
432) As in LXI. GoM doesn't mention her name.
433) As in GoM (9:9). LXI = *Gwalchmai*.
434) LXI = *Yrien*. GoM (9:9) = *Urian*.
435) As in GoM (9:9). LXI = *Reged*.
436) As in GoM (9:9). LXI = *Gwenhwyfar*.
437) *Gogvran* is not mentioned in GoM. Instead, GoM (9:9) speaks of her as the daughter of a Roman noble but that she had been raised in Cador's household. The word translated here as 'mighty' is *kawr*, which simply means 'great' or 'exalted', but is often translated as 'giant' as in Jones, 1929. Griscom (p. 545) thinks that *Gogvran the Prince* "would not be inaccurate."
438) LXI = *Isslont*, which GoM (9:10) translates as Iceland. It should read *Islay*. The early medieval Welsh knew Iceland as *ynys yr ia* (still its name in modern Welsh), but Islay as *Islont*. Griscom's note (pp. 545-6) is most instructive on this point.
439) As in LXI. GoM (9:10) = *Doldavius*.
440) As in LXI. GoM (9:10) = *Gunhpar*.

prowess in battle and that of his comrades, as well for his heroism as for his liberal laws and usages, for this land had never seen the like. Nor could any king in those days be likened to Arthur, for every king feared him lest he should make war against him. And when Arthur heard the things that were said of him, he desired to match that praise with [valorous] deeds. And he thought to have conquered all Europe, the third part of all the world. And there was neither king nor mighty lord who did not try to learn the ways and manners of Arthur and his court.

And then Arthur prepared a fleet to go to Lochland, for Sichelm,[441] king of Prydyn,[442] had died and had bequeathed the throne to Loth,[443] the son of Kynvarch, his nephew. But the men of Lochland would have none of it, and elected Riculf[444] their king. And they fortified their strongholds to defend their land. And in that place was Gawain, the son of Loth, in the pay of the bishop of Rome,[445] to whom Arthur, his uncle, had sent him to learn the manners and usages and horsemanship of the Romans. And the bishop [of Rome] it was who first conferred knighthood upon Gawain.

And when Arthur was come to Lochland, there was Riculf with a mighty army to oppose him. And they gave battle, with many falling on either side. But at the last, Arthur slew Riculf and annexed the whole country to himself along with Denmark, and he forced the people to pay him fealty. And he left Loth, the son of Kynvarch, as king over these lands, and from thence did Arthur sail with his fleet to Gaul to subdue it. And to face him came Frollo,[446] who was lord of Gaul under Leo,[447] the emperor of Rome. And he fought against Arthur but could not subdue him, for Arthur's mounted knights were too numerous and skilful for him. So Frollo took flight to Paris where he mustered the greatest army that he could.

---

441) As in GoM (9:11). LXI = *Assychlym*.
442) Again, GoM (9:11) erroneously translates this as Norway. *Prydain*, or *Prydyn*, was the country around Loch Lomond (it is synonymous with *Llychlyn*, Loch Land, the west coast of Scotland), and was never part of Norway in spite of the fact that *Llychlyn* is the modern Welsh for Scandinavia.
443) As in GoM (9:11). LXI = *Llew*.
444) As in GoM (9:11). LXI = *Rikwlff*.
445) GoM (9:11) = *Pope Sulpicius*. No pope of that precise name is known, which indicates a certain illegibility in the source document. However, the reference may refer to Pope Silverius who reigned for just nine months between June 8th 536 to March 11th 537, the date of his deposition according to the *Annuario Pontifico*. If correct, this enables us to narrow down the chronology of these events dramatically.
446) As in GoM (9:11). LXI = *ffrolo*.
447) As in LXI and GoM (9:11).

And Arthur enclosed that city for a month so that many within perished from hunger. And then was Frollo deeply troubled, and he put it to Arthur that both of them should go to an island in the river Seine,[448] the same which runs through the midst of the city of Paris, and that he who prevails should take the other's kingdom but leave the armies in peace. And Arthur consented to what he said. And so they went together to the island armed and mounted, with their two armies looking on. And Frollo straightway attacked Arthur with his spear, but Arthur avoided the danger. And without [further] ado, Arthur charged at Frollo, knocking him under his horse's belly and drawing his sword in an attempt to kill him. But Frollo got bravely to his feet and slew Arthur's horse so that Arthur and his horse tumbled to the ground. And the Britons on seeing it, were hard pressed to keep their peace with the Gauls.

And Arthur, filled with anger, stood up and swung his shield around so that it hung between himself and Frollo, and then he closed with him, and they exchanged mighty sword strokes between them. And with his sword, Frollo struck Arthur upon the forehead so that the blood gushed to the ground down his face and breast. But Arthur, moved to fury, lifted Excalibur aloft and brought it down upon the crown of Frollo's head, cleaving his body and his armour to the waist. And there did Frollo fall, scoring the turf with his heels till death took him.

And the whole of Gaul paid fealty to Arthur, and Arthur divided his host into two. The one half he sent to his nephew Howel, to conquer the Poitevins.[449] And taking the other to himself, he went off to war against Gascony[450] and Anjou.[451] And Guitard,[452] lord of the Poitevins, was forced to pay fealty to Arthur, and Arthur spent nine years in conquering those lands.

And after these things, he held his court in Paris to where he summoned all the lords of the isles and the nobles, [both] lay and clergy. And with the consent of all who were gathered there, there were established good laws for every one of these nations. And Arthur bestowed upon Bedevere,[453] his chief butler, the earldom of Normandy. And to Kay,[454] his chief steward, the earldom of

---

448) LXI = *ssain*. The river is not named in GoM.
449) LXI = *peitio*.
450) LXI = *Gassgwin*.
451) LXI = *Einssio*. GoM (9:11) = *Aquitania*.
452) As in GoM (9:11). LXI = *Gwidrad*.
453) As in GoM (10:6). LXI = *Bedwyr*.
454) LXI = *Kei*.

Anjou,[455] and [lands to] all his other servants according to their worthiness. And by his liberality and love he united them in peace.

And when he had settled all things, he returned the following spring to the land of Britain. And he was advised by [his] council to hold court at Caerleon-on-Usk, for that was the most noble and enriched of all his cities, the fittest in which to hold court. For on one side of the city there is a great river upon which ships from the ends of the earth can sail. Whilst on the other side of the city, there are lovely meadows, level and dry. And around [all] these are majestic hills with forests great and green and in which much game may be had. And in the city [itself] were buildings of royal worth, for whose sake the place was compared to Rome.

And there were, besides, two great churches in the city, one of them being dedicated to the memory of Silvius the Martyr,[456] wherein was a convent of nuns, and the other was dedicated to Aaron the Martyr, which was a monastic house of canons. And in this place was also the third most important arch-diocese in the realm. And there were, moreover, two hundred clerical schools in the city, given to all kinds of learning. And such is Caerleon-on-Usk, the principal city in the land, where Arthur held a great and marvellous feast. And he sent envoys to every land he had conquered to summon all their kings, chiefs and ministers, such numbers of them that they could not be counted, to come to Caerleon[-on-Usk] to share the feast. And he commanded that all should receive honours according to their lineage, their dignity and their rank.

And from Albany came Aron, son of Kynvarch and lord of Prydyn. And Urien, son of Kynvarch and lord of Moray. And Casswallon [surnamed] Longhand, lord of Gwynedd,[457] and Mayric, king of Dyfed. And Cador, earl of Cornwall,[458] and the three archbishops of the land of Britain, chief among whom was the archbishop of Caerleon-on-Usk, for he was the [pope's] legate, a saintly man. And there was also Morvid, earl of Gloucester,[459] and Mor, the earl of Worcester.[460] And Anarawd, lord of Shrewsbury,[461] and Madoc of

---

455) LXI = *Angiw.*
456) LXI = *ssiliws.* GoM (9:12) = *Julius the Martyr.*
457) LXI = *Kasswallawn Lawhir.* GoM (9:12) = *Cadwallo Laurh,* king of the Venedoti.
458) GoM (9:12) adds *Soter* to this list, the king of the *Demetae* or South Welsh.
459) As in GoM (9:12). LXI = *Morydd Kaerloyw.*
460) LXI = *Kaer rangon,* Worcester. GoM (9:12) = *Mauron,* earl of Worcester.
461) LXI = *amwythic.* GoM (9:12) translates this name as Salisbury, but see note 463.

Warwick.[462] And Owen of Salisbury,[463] and Gwrssalen of Dorchester,[464] and Urien of Bath,[465] and Bosso, earl of Oxford.[466] And with these many others, whom I shall not name for weariness.

And from other lands there came Gillomaur, king of Ireland. And another Gillomaur, lord of Islay,[467] and Doldaf, king of Scotland. And Gwynnwas, lord of the Orkneys, and Loth, son of Kynvarch and king of Lochland. And Achel, king of the Danes. And from the land of Gaul came Oldin, lord of the Ruteni,[468] and Borellus, lord of Maine,[469] Leodegar of Boulogne,[470] and Bedevere, earl of Normandy. And Kay, prince of Anjou, and Guitard, king of the Poitevins. And the twelve peers [of Gaul], with Geraint of Chartres over them. And Howel, the son of Ambrosius of Armorica, with many others whom time renders nameless.

And there never came to any feast before such an array of noblemen and noblewomen, fine horses, hawks, hounds, precious jewels, golden dishes and rich attire of satin and purple as came there that day. And there was not an ambitious man this side of Spain who did not attend the feast and receive gifts without number -whatever he desired! And many came uninvited, just to gaze upon it all.

And when all had gathered together, the three archbishops were ordained to clothe the king in his regal attire and to place the crown upon his head. And as they entered the church, two of the archbishops led Arthur in his kingly gown, and before him went four knights bearing unsheathed swords, which was the dignity accorded only to an emperor. And the four knights were Aron, son of Kynvarch [and] king of Albany, and Casswallon [surnamed] Longhand, lord of Gwynedd, and Mayric, king of Dyfed, and Cador, earl of Cornwall. And on either side of these there sang the convent choirs, singing anthems to the accompaniment of organs, the best and sweetest music that ever was chanted.

And the queen went to the other church in her queenly attire, wearing her crown upon her head and accompanied by bishops and nuns, with the four

---

462) LXI = *kaer Wair*. GoM (9:12) = *Guerensis* (of Warwick).
463) LXI = *kaer Vallawc*, which is explained in the text as being *ssaltsbri*. GoM, however, (see note 461) erroneously identifies *Amwythic* as Salisbury. GoM, being himself a native of Wales, would surely have known the difference had his text been eligible and clear.
464) LXI = *kaer Kynnvarch*, i.e. Dorchester. GoM (9:12) = *Caistor*.
465) LXI = *kaer Vaddon*. GoM (9:12) = *Urbgennius of Bath*.
466) LXI = *Rydychen*.
467) LXI = *Alawnt*, a possible variant for Islay. Not mentioned in GoM.
468) LXI = *Rwytton*, the *Ruteni* of southern Gaul.
469) LXI = *Kenonia*, i.e. Maine. GoM (9:12) = *Borellus of Cenomania*.
470) LXI = *Bolwyn*, i.e. Boulogne. GoM (9:12) = *Leodegarius of Hoiland*.

wives of the princes [who were waiting upon the king], each bearing a white pigeon in her hand. And when she, the queen, had entered the church, the monks opened the service with the sweetest anthems that ever were sung, and there was much hurrying to and fro [by the onlookers] between the churches, that they might hear the wondrous singing.

And after the Eucharist, they, the king and queen, went to the palace, and laying aside their regal apparel they put on other garments and went to the hall to eat. And Guinevere sat with her noble ladies apart from the rest, which was the queenly custom [in those days]. And when he had allotted to all their several places according to their dignity, so Kay arose wearing a robe of yellow ermine, with a thousand servants to help him who were likewise attired. And with him rose Bedevere, Arthur's chief butler, with a thousand servants dressed in his livery, and they served yellow mead in gold and silver cups without number. And neither the number nor the attire of the queen's servants were less than those of the king.

And there was not a kingdom that could be likened to the land of Britain for wealth, ceremonial or custom. And one law was followed by all the men of Arthur's court, and their wives had but one manner of dress. Neither would dame nor damsel take as husband or sweetheart any who was not a proven and a worthy knight. And for this [cause] were the men the more gallant and the women the more chaste. And having dined, all went outside the city to see the jousting and other sports, for every game that could be thought of was being played there. And the ladies watched from the battlements of the city, from whence each of them showed which knight she favoured most. And for this cause did each man perform the bravest deed he could. And whosoever emerged victorious from the games, was awarded prizes for his labours, each at the cost of the king's treasury.

And after three days and three nights of such festivities, it was enacted on the fourth day that each who had given service would be rewarded for his deeds. And to some were given cities, and to others were given castles, and to others any bishoprics that lay vacant.

And then Dubricius, archbishop of Caerleon-on-Usk, lay aside his archbishopric and declared himself a hermit, for he had witnessed all the extravagance of the feast and of the multitude who attended it, and how all was spent and done in but three short days. And he thought upon the end that awaits all worldly vanities, and he sought things that never perish, reaching forward towards the Kingdom of Heaven.

And in his stead was David,[471] the son of Samson, made archbishop, for he was a man of saintly conversation - and an uncle of Arthur. And to replace Samson, archbishop of Eboracum, there came Tailo,[472] the bishop of Llandaff. And this was at the bidding of Howel, the son of Ambrosius of Armorica, for Tailo [too was deemed] a saintly man.

And when all these things were accomplished, behold, there drew near twelve nobles of high dignity, each of whom bore an olive branch in his hand as a token of their embassy. And they saluted Arthur with much ceremony and gave him greetings from Lucius,[473] emperor of Rome. And they placed a letter into his hands which said this: "Lucius, emperor of Rome, sends greetings to Arthur, king of the Britons, according to his merits. For your viciousness and foolishness, nay your irrational folly, all amaze me! You have insulted the Roman empire and are too sluggish in paying her tribute, even though the kings of all the earth bow down to her. But you - you have withheld the tribute due to Rome from the land of Britain, won by Julius Caesar and other emperors after him! All other nations pay tribute to Rome, but you have taken the land of Britain for yourself, tarnishing the good name of the Romans. And for this cause does the Roman Senate summon you to Rome to be here by August, to receive judgment upon you according to their will. And [therefore have these ambassadors] come to so summon you. But and if you will not come at the set time, then be it known to you that the Romans will come to Britain to claim recompense of you for your insult to Rome - and the sword shall judge between us!"

And when Arthur perceived the intent of the letter, he sought counsel as to what answer he should give the Romans. And first rose Cador, earl of Cornwall, who said to the king, "My liege, I fear that luxury and indolence have sapped the manliness from us Britons, because we have wasted ourselves in idleness and feasting, gossiping like women these five years past. This has stripped us of our courage and manliness. We [therefore] should thank the Romans for rousing us [to our old selves again]."

And Arthur replied, "My lords and comrades in arms, you have ever before this given me sound and profitable counsel, of the which I have need in this hour. Let us therefore think well on this, and if our conclusions be right, then

---

471) As in GoM (9:15). LXI = *Dewi*. GoM does not give his father's name, merely calling him Arthur's uncle. Whether David's father was the brother of Gorlois or an as yet unnamed brother of Uther Pendragon is not stated in either version.

472) As in LXI. GoM (9:15) = *Tebaus*.

473) LXI = *Lles*. GoM (9:15) = *Lucius Hiberius*. GoM describes him as Procurator of the Republic.

we shall prevail over the Romans. Now, whilst they truly did receive tribute from this land for providing us with legions with which they defended us from [those] foreign invaders, [the Picts and the Saxons], they no longer do so. Then seeing that they demand of us something that we do not owe them, so let us demand of them what they owe us, [namely, defence against our foes in return for this tribute], and may the strongest take tribute from the other! [And remember], our ancestors, Belinus and Brennus, the sons of Dunvallo Molmutius, vanquished them. And they brought back to the land of Britain twenty Roman nobles as hostages. And after them, Constantine, the son of Helen and the great Maximianus, nobles all of the land of Britain, they conquered as far as Rome and even Rome herself besides, and ruled there as emperors one after another. So for these reasons, let us give them no answer save only to demand of them [the tribute] that they owe us!"

And then spoke Howel, the son of Ambrosius of Armorica, saying, "Let God be witness, if every man here were to tell his thoughts in turn, there would be heard no better words than those spoken by our king. Therefore, my liege, let us stir ourselves and defend the honour of our land, for seeing that the Romans ask unlawful things of us, then it is for you, sire, to demand rightful things of them. The wise Sybil[474] once foretold that there were to be three emperors from Kymry ruling Rome. Now, there have already been two,[475] and you shall be the third. Let us therefore make haste, for all your people share your mind, and I myself shall give you ten thousand knights in support!"

And at that spoke Aron, son of Kynvarch, saying, "Let God be witness, my liege, words cannot tell how great is my joy over what you have spoken concerning Rome. And we are content therefore to receive blows from Rome in return for those that we shall deal her, that we might avenge our grandfathers and more ancient forebears. And to uphold your royal dignity, my liege, I shall give two thousand mounted knights, and foot soldiers also!"

And when all had done with speaking and had told how many warriors each would give to war against Rome, Arthur thanked them all every one for their support. And then was reckoned to Arthur the great number of warriors [that had been] promised him. And they were, from the land of Britain sixty thousand mounted knights well proven in battle, besides those promised him by Howel, and foot soldiers beyond reckoning. And from the six lands of Ireland, Islay, Scotland, the Orkneys, Lochland and Denmark, one hundred and twenty thousand foot soldiers. And of the whole of Gaul he would receive eighty

---

474) LXI = *ssibli*, the Sybilline prophecies. This reference doesn't appear in GoM's version of Cador's speech.
475) Referring to Belinus and Constantine I.

thousand mounted knights. And from the twelve peers [of Gaul] and Geraint of Chartres,[476] would come one thousand two hundred armed warriors. And the entire number that was promised was about ninety-two thousand two hundred mounted knights,[477] and foot soldiers without number.

And when Arthur had seen every man's zeal, he sent messages [throughout his domains] that [all men should prepare themselves] for August. And he informed the Roman envoys [that he would indeed be in Rome for August, as the emperor asked], but not [so] that he would pay them tribute. And with that the envoys went away. And when Lucius, the emperor of Rome, heard of it, he sought counsel from the Senate of Rome, and their counsel was to seek help against Arthur from the kings of the east. And the number of soldiers that Lucius, emperor of Rome, was given, was a hundred and forty-four thousand.[478] And when all was ready and August was near, they set out towards the land of Britain.

And when news of this came to Arthur, he mustered his forces and gave to his nephew Mordred,[479] his sister's son, the rule of his kingdom for safekeeping, and Guinevere to guard well until he should return. And then Arthur went with his army to the port of Southampton,[480] and at the rising of a favourable wind he sailed to Gaul. But when he was half way across the channel, a sleep such as the dead enjoy fell upon him for most of the night, and he dreamed a dream. And he saw rising from the south a flying dragon, landing upon the shore of Gaul with a mighty scream. And he saw [in his dream] another dragon coming from the west, and the sea shone from the glow of its eyes. And he saw this dragon making war against [the constellation of] the Bear [whose name amongst the Britons was Arth]. And when the battle had raged for some time, he saw the dragon spewing out fire over the Bear, consuming him utterly in its flames. And Arthur was deeply troubled by the dream. And when he awoke, he

---

476) LXI = *Kaerwys*, Chartres.
477) GoM (9:19) gives 183,300, not counting infantry. This suggests illegibility in the original source (see Thorpe, p. 235).
478) The text of LXI translates literally as "...a hundred and forty and four hundred thousand of thousands" (!), at which point the Welsh translator is clearly in difficulties with his source material. It implies illegibility at the very least. GoM fares no better. He gives 400,160 for Lucius' army.
479) As in GoM (10:2). LXI = *Medrod*.
480) LXI = *Northamtwn*, but see note 417. Porth has again been misread as north by the medieval translator. Arthur would have had great difficulty in sailing a fleet out of the real Northampton, though it is equally hard to imagine that a Welsh scholar would have been so ignorant of Northampton's geographical location.

told of what he had seen to his comrades, and this was their interpretation: "You, O king, shall do battle with a monstrous giant and overcome it, for the dragon portended yourself!" But Arthur gave it no credence, for he sensed that [he might lose the battle] between the emperor and himself.

And by the following day Arthur came with his fleet to the port of Barfleur[481] in Normandy.

And there he awaited the coming of all the warriors that had been promised by his domains. And then came news to Arthur that Lucius, emperor of Rome, was encamped with a mighty host upon the opposite bank of the river Aube.[482] And in the night Arthur made camp on the other side of the river, and Arthur sent heralds to the emperor telling him that either he must relinquish Gaul and all its borders, or give him open battle the day following. And the heralds who were sent there were Gawain, son of Gwyar, and Bosso, earl of Oxford, and Geraint of Chartres, prince of Gaul. And Arthur's host were mighty glad of Geraint being there, for they suspected he would find a way of goading the Romans into battle.

And Lucius was told of the coming of the heralds and the nature of their message, and he answered that it was better for him to conquer Gaul than to surrender it. And Caius,[483] who was nephew to the emperor, said, "[I have heard tell that] the tongues of you Britons are longer than your swords!" And hearing it, Gawain straightway drew his sword and slew Caius. And they, the three heralds, quickly remounted their steeds with the Romans in pursuit of them, seeking to avenge [the slaying of Caius] upon them. Then Geraint, who was in the rear, wounded and killed the leader of those giving chase. And Marcellus Mutius[484] drew near to avenge Caius, and Gawain waited for him and struck him on the head with his sword, splitting him down to the bone. And he bade him tell his fellows in hell that the swords of the Britons are longer than their tongues! And at Gawain's further bidding, they, the heralds, stayed together and each slew a leader of those giving chase.[485]

And as they came close to a wood, behold, six thousand Britons raised a battle cry against the Romans and slew them without mercy. Others they

---

481) As in GoM (10:2). LXI = *Barilio*.
482) As in GoM (10:4). LXI = *Gwenn*.
483) LXI = *Keiws*. GoM (10:4) = *Gaius Quintillanus*.
484) As in GoM (10:4). LXI = *Markinigys*.
485) Here is a rare mention of the typical fighting tactics of the Britons, which Julius Caesar describes in some detail and which his soldiers found so unnerving.

captured and put the remainder to flight. And when Petreius,[486] a Roman senator, learned of it, he went forward with ten thousand soldiers to defend [his fellow] Romans. And at the first charge, he drove the Britons back into the wood where they had been waiting, and there were many slain on either side.

And then Edyrn, the son of Nydd,[487] came with five thousand warriors to help the Britons. And they, the Romans, resisted them heroically, thus attesting their renown and pride. And Petreius exhorted his soldiers to fight with valour. And when Bosso, earl of Oxford, saw it, he mustered together many warriors and went out against them, calling to Gawain who was close by, "Take heed that we be not defeated and blamed by the king, and let us try to defeat Petreius either by killing him or capturing him!" And straightway they broke through the ranks of the Roman army and pulled Petreius from his horse, binding him fast. And the battle was fierce on either side, but at the last the Britons won the day and took Petreius with them back to their own ranks. And the Romans renewed the battle and at last caused the Britons to flee, and they captured, killed and plundered as they pleased.

And then the Britons came with their prisoners into Arthur's presence and told him all that had come to pass. And Arthur rejoiced exceedingly that they had done as much whilst he himself was not there [to lead them]. And Arthur delegated Bedevere and Cador, earl of Cornwall, and two other nobles to convey the prisoners to Paris. And when the Romans knew of it, they selected fifteen thousand soldiers to go at dead of night and effect the release of the prisoners. And leading that force were Quintus Milvius,[488] a senator of Rome, Ofander, commander of the Syrian Legion,[489] and Sertorius, a Lybian.[490] And they lay in wait [for the Britons] in a secret place.

And the following day, as Arthur's men came with their prisoners to the wooded valley in which the Romans were waiting, they, the Romans, fell upon them and scattered them. Then the Britons split up into two divisions, the one headed by Bedevere and Richard[491] of Baldwin to keep the prisoners, and the

---

486) LXI = *Pentaraink*. GoM (10:4) = *Petreius Cocta*.
487) As in LXI. GoM (10:4) = *Hyderus*, the son of *Nu*.
488) LXI = *Achwintys*. GoM (10:5) = *Quintus Carucius*. GoM states that Quintus was accompanied by *Vulteius Catellus*.
489) As in LXI. GoM (10:5) = *Evander*, king of Syria. This reference, along with that to the king of Lybia, is a most telling piece of evidence for the authenticity of the chronicle. For a discussion of these and other points, see *After the Flood*.
490) As in GoM (10:5). LXI = *ssertorys*.
491) LXI = *Rissiart*. GoM (10:4) = *Richerius*.

other lead by Cador, earl of Cornwall, and the lord Borel. And the Romans fell upon them, but there then came Guitard, lord of the Poitevins, with three thousand warriors to help the Britons. And they, the Britons and the Poitevins, bravely battled with the Romans and repaid their deceit and treachery. And the lord Borel was slain in that place, for Ofander, the Syrian commander, pierced him with a javelin so that he died. And four others of Arthur's men were slain, namely Hirlas of Eliawn,[492] and Mayric, son of Cador, and Halidyc of Tintagel,[493] and Kay, son of Ithel. But for all that adversity, the Britons lost not a prisoner amongst them, but put the Romans to flight. And in that flight was Ofander, commander of the Syrian legion, killed, as also was Vulteius Catellus, a Roman knight.

And having won the day, the Britons took their prisoners to Paris, along with those who had been captured that day. And with joy they returned to Arthur and recounted all that had happened. And Lucius was greatly troubled at the evil fortunes befalling his men, and he held council as to whether he should send to Rome for more help, or alone face a battle with Arthur. And in the council it was ordained that they, the Romans, [should] head through Nivernais[494] for the town of Langres,[495] where they might pass the night.

And when Arthur knew of it, he went [with his army] to a place called the Vale of Saussy,[496] for Lucius the emperor must come through there the following day. And Arthur awaited him there and stationed his cavalry on either side, with Morvid, earl of Gloucester, to command them. And he divided his army into eight divisions, and in each division were three thousand five hundred proven warriors.[497] And having wisely instructed them, Arthur commanded them both to attack and also to wait [as necessary]. And at the head of each division were two commanders, well known for their prowess [in battle]. Commanding the first were Aron, son of Kynvarch, and Cador, earl of Cornwall. And that division was stationed to the right. And commanding the other on the left flank were Bosso of Oxford and Geraint of Chartres. Heading the third division were Achel, lord of the Danes, and Loth, son of Kynvarch and

---

492) As in LXI. GoM (10:5) = *Hyrelgas of Periron*.
493) As in LXI. GoM (10:5) = *Aliduc of Tintagel*.
494) LXI = *Nafarn*. GoM (10:6) = *Autun*. The close knowledge of Gaulish geography is a telling and unexpected feature of this British chronicle.
495) As in GoM (10:6). LXI = *Leigrys*.
496) LXI = *Anssessia*, Saussy, as in GoM (10:6). This place lies some thirty-five miles south-west of Langres. For a discussion of the geography, see Thorpe, p. 247.
497) GoM (10:6) has 5,555, implying illegibility.

lord of Prydyn. And leading the fourth were Howel, the son of Ambrosius of Armorica, and Gawain, son of Gwyar.

And at the rear were posted four other divisions with two commanders to lead each of them. The first was commanded by Kay [surnamed] Longfellow, and Bedevere, son of Bedrod. And leading the second were Holdin, lord of the Ruteni, and Guitard, prince of the Poitevins. And commanding the third were Owen of Caerleon and Gwynnwas of Canterbury. And over the fourth were placed Urien of Bath and Gwrssalen of Dorchester. And bringing up the rear were Arthur and a host of knights with him. And ahead of him was carried the Golden Dragon [of his father, Uther], to which all [who were] wounded might retreat. And Arthur's own division consisted of some six thousand three hundred men.[498]

And Arthur encouraged his men [to battle] with these words, "My lords, it is known to all men that it was by your might and wisdom that the land of Britain came to be supreme over thirty kingdoms. And by that same might [and wisdom] shall we prevail over Rome and wreak vengeance upon them for hoping to bring us into servitude rather than freedom. And call [you] to mind in this hour that idle peace in which we lived for so long - trading gossip with housewives! And remember, moreover, to summon up again your courage and knightly skills. And let us be of one mind when we encounter the Romans and round them up like sheep, for they do not believe that we have courage enough to engage them in open battle. And if you do altogether as I have commanded you, my lords, then shall I bestow honours upon you and anything else that it is in my power to give!"

And they vowed, every one, to do altogether as Arthur had commanded them. And when Lucius heard that Arthur had addressed his soldiers, he also admonished his men, telling them that all the earth should be subject to Rome, and [he said], "Remember that your ancestors made Rome the mistress of the world by their courage, their skill in battle and their good fortune. And neither shall you shrink even from death to maintain the dignity of Rome. Fight well, that we might win tribute from other lands also. And bear this in mind, that we did not come here to flee, but as one man to fight our foes. And although they may look as though they ought to be feared, yet shall we overcome them!"

And when he had finished, he divided his army into twelve divisions, and with each division he placed a legion of cavalry. And to lead each division there were two trusty commanders. And Lucius instructed his men in whatever they needed to know, and in the midst of the host he commanded to be raised the Golden Eagle as a rallying point for any who were wounded in battle.

---

498) GoM (10:6) has 6,666.

And they, the opposing armies, gave battle, and at the beginning the Spanish legion [of the Romans] encountered the division led by Aron, son of Kynvarch, and Cador, earl of Cornwall. And fierce was the battle that ensued. And Geraint of Chartres and Bosso of Oxford came up [with their division] and penetrated the Roman ranks. And from that moment, they clashed so furiously and amid such confusion that the ground trembled and the skies echoed with [the din of battle] and of men stamping their feet upon the ground [in their march]. And the fighting was so fierce on either side that it would be wearisome to recount [it all]. And in that battle did Bocchus, the Median commander, run Bedevere through with a javelin and slew him. And Kay also was wounded unto death. But for all that, they, the Britons of his division, bore his body until they encountered the Lybian host who put them to flight. But they carried his body back to the Golden Dragon.

And then Hirlas, the nephew of Bedevere, led three hundred valorous and war-hungry knights in a charge like that of a wild boar amongst a pack of hounds. And he continued to charge at them until he encountered Bocchus, and him he carried off with him on horseback until they drew nigh to Bedevere's body. And there he, Bocchus, was hewn in pieces. And Hirlas returned to his own ranks and exhorted them to slaughter the foe. And multitudes fell on either side.

And amongst the Roman soldiery there were slain Ali Fatima [of the Lybian host], and Quintus Milvius, knight. And amongst Arthur's men there were slain Holdin, lord of the Ruteni, and Leodegar of Boulogne. And three other nobles also [were slain], namely Gwrssalen of Canterbury, Gwalhoc of Salisbury, and Urien of Bath. And Kay died also from an earlier wound. And then the warriors in the front line of battle fell back to the ranks of Howel, the son of Ambrosius of Armorica, and Gawain. And in doing so they were strengthened and bravely renewed the onslaught upon their foes. And whoever encountered Gawain was slain by a single stroke [of his sword]. Nor did Gawain refrain [from battle] until he had penetrated to the very guard of the Roman emperor.

And it was there that the Britons suffered loss by the slaying of Kynvarch, lord of Treguier,[499] and two thousand [of his men] with him. And three other nobles[500] [also] were slain in that place, whose courage was worthy of a king. And Howel and Gawain held their ranks and maintained their worth, slaying whomsever they encountered, dealing and receiving blows. And at last Gawain got his dearest wish and encountered Lucius, emperor of Rome. And Lucius

---

499) LXI = *Teyger*. GoM (10:10) = *Chinmarchocus, duke of Treguier*.
500) Named by GoM (10:10) as *Riddomarcus, Bloctonius,* and *Iaginvius of Bodloan*.

was glad of it and they fought together. And when the battle was at its height, there fell upon Howel and Gawain['s division a fresh body of] Roman troops, so that they fell back to Arthur's ranks [for safety]. And when Arthur saw it, he was filled with wrath and charged the Roman lines, waving Excalibur at them and shouting to his men, "Make haste, my lords, to right the wrongs that your ancestors suffered under these arrogant [Romans]. Strike fearlessly at them and summon your might as ever you have done, and let us not retreat from them a single step!"

And leading his warriors, Arthur savaged the foe like a raging lion, and whomsoever he met he slew them with a single stroke [of Excalibur, his sword]. And all fled from him like animals from a ravenous lion, for no armour afforded protection against his blows. And Arthur encountered two commanders, Sertorius of the Lybian host, and Poltetes of the Bythinian. And he slew them both with two single strokes. And when all the Britons beheld their lord prevailing, they fought heroically as after the example of their king.

And the Romans did likewise, exhorting and threatening their men. And those who were slain on either side were beyond reckoning. And then Morvid, earl of Gloucester, moved up with a host of knights and renewed the onslaught against the Romans. And one of the Britons slew Lucius, emperor of Rome, with a javelin, so that he fell dead to the earth.[501] But it was not known who slew him. And the Britons prevailed and put the Romans to flight, slaying and hacking at them for trying to compel free men to pay them tribute. And Arthur commanded the Britons to separate the bodies of his fallen from those of the Romans, and to bury them with honour in the nearest monasteries. And Arthur commanded also that the Roman dead be sent for burial amongst their [own] comrades.

And the body of Bedevere was carried into Normandy to the city that he himself had founded, and there was he buried. And the body of Kay was carried to Poitiers, and it was buried there within a church of hermits. And Holdin, lord of the Ruteni, was borne to Flanders, and all other noble dead were carried to the nearest churches [for burial]. And Arthur commanded that the body of the Roman emperor be laid before the Senate of Rome as a warning not

---

501) I could find no reference to this character.

to return to the Britons a second time seeking tribute. And Arthur remained where he was that he might subdue all Burgundy.

And as Arthur set out during the first week of summer to cross the high Alps[502] on his way to Rome, he was approached by runners from the land of Britain who told him that Mordred, his nephew, the son of his sister, had usurped the crown of the realm, had taken Guinevere into his bed as [if she were] his wedded wife, and had taken the kingdom [to himself]. And Arthur hurried toward Britain, leaving Howel, the son of Ambrosius of Armorica, to lay waste the Roman dominions. And Mordred was compelled [by this] to send Chelric[503] to invite the Germans to come to Britain with the mightiest host they could gather. And [he told them that] he would bestow upon them what Vortigern had bestowed upon them, from the Humber to the shire of Kent.

Then went Chelric to Germany, and he returned again with seven hundred[504] longships filled with armed pagans. And whilst he awaited their arrival, Mordred made an alliance with the Picts, the Scots and the Irish - indeed with any people who despised Arthur - until his host numbered eighty thousand warriors. And Mordred journeyed with his host down to Southampton[505] to try to prevent Arthur's landing [his troops there]. And on both sides were multitudes slain, foremost of whom were Aron, son of Kynvarch, and Gawain, son of Gwyar. And in Aron's command was placed Urien, son of Kynvarch, [his brother]. And by a mighty act, [but at the loss of many of his] nobles, Arthur made land, compelling Mordred to flee and scattering his men. And as night fell, Mordred rallied his men together and marched [with them] to Winchester, to fortify the city against Arthur and his men. And when news of it reached Guinevere, she betook herself to Caerleon where she donned a nun's habit and joined the sisters of the church of Silvius the Martyr.

And after three days, when he had buried his dead, Arthur came with his host to Winchester, and Mordred sallied forth with his host from the city and gave battle to Arthur, and each side suffered a mighty slaughter. But at last Mordred fell back and fled to Cornwall. And Arthur did not wait [this time] to bury his dead, but gave chase to the traitor Mordred, angry that he had twice

---

502) LXI = *mynyddoedd Mynnav*.
503) As in GoM (11:1). LXI = *Selix*.
504) GoM (11:1) has eight hundred ships.
505) LXI = *Norddhamtwn*, another misreading of Porth Hamon (see notes 417 and 480). Curiously, GoM (11:1) has Arthur landing at Richborough.

escaped him. And then, on the river Camlann,[506] Mordred lay in wait for Arthur, and the number of Mordred's host was sixty thousand six hundred and six. And he, Mordred, deemed it more prudent to lie in wait for Arthur than to flee the place. And Mordred divided his men into nine legions, and he promised to all that he would bestow upon them - should he be victorious - more lands, treasures and other gifts than their hearts could desire.

And then Arthur exhorted his own men to fight well against him [in these words]: "My lords, yonder host could never fight in unison, for they are a mercenary and a babbling host of heathens. They have not the same resolve as [we] good Christians. And right is on our side, but evil on theirs!"

And thus leading his men, Arthur gave battle to his foes. And he and his host fought with such anger that those [of the enemy] who lived, were driven insane by the wails and lamentations of the dying. And when evening was drawing nigh, Arthur fell upon Mordred's own legion and scattered them, thoroughly penetrating [their defences]. And this much did Arthur as a lion in the midst of sheep. And in that charge he slew Mordred and thousands with him. Yet the greatest battle that ever was fought, was fought that day even though Mordred was now dead.

And amongst the dead of Mordred's host were these. Of the Saxon [lords], Elaf, Egbriht and Bruning.[507] Of the Irish [chieftains], Gillomaur, Gilpatrick, Gillasel and Gillaurus. And all the Pictish and Scottish lords were slain.

And among [those of] Arthur's [dead were numbered] Ebras, king of Lochland, Achel, lord of the Danes, Cador [surnamed] Lemmenic, and Casswallon, and thousands more besides. And Arthur also received a deadly wound, and from the midst of [the battle of] Camlann he was taken to the Isle of Avalon to be healed. [But of such things] there is no more [to be found] written here than this.[508] And to Constantine, the son of Cador, did Arthur

---

506) LXI = *kamlan*. To which Thorpe (p. 259) adds: "On 4th August 1960 I visited Camelford [in Cornwall] and walked along the River Camel as far as Slaughter Bridge.... [where] I found an ancient stone.... The stone was uneven and broken, and the letters were straggling and irregular, but the following fragment of an inscription was clearly to be deciphered: LATIN...IIC IACIT FILIVS M...AR... = possibly 'Latinus hic iacet filius Merlini Arturus.' In *Corpus Inscriptionem Insularium Celticarum*, R A S Macalister, 1945, Vol. I, pp. 447-9, it is transcribed as LATINI IC IACIT FILIVS MAGARI, with an Ogham inscription LA[T]INI at the top end."
507) As in GoM (11:2). LXI = *Eiaes, Brytt*, and *Bwfynt*, respectively.
508) This is a direct reference to the original source book that the Welsh translator was using, and which seems to have been common to both himself and Geoffrey of Monmouth, who, however, omits this editorial comment. The comment seems to convey either a disappointment on the translator's part, or an apology to the reader who may be expecting something more from the text. At any rate, the original source material evidently contained nothing of the later legendary embellishments that surrounded the death and hoped-for return of Arthur.

bequeath the crown and the realm. And the year of Christ was five hundred and forty-two.[509]

And at this place ends the history of Arthur and Mordred

And when Constantine had been anointed king, there rose up against him the two sons of Mordred and the Saxons. But it availed them nothing. And at that time died David, archbishop of Caerleon-on-Usk. And Maelgwn, [lord of] Gwynedd,[510] commanded him to be buried with honour. And after many battles between Constantine and the Saxons, the Saxons fled with the sons of Mordred to London. [And one of the sons of Mordred] was slain there, [cowering] in a monastery. And the other son sought refuge in Winchester, where he was slain before the high altar of the church of Amphibalus.[511] And in the third year[512] of his reign, was Constantine slain by the mighty Conan.

And he was laid to rest next to Uther Pendragon in the Giant's Ring at Salisbury. And there reigned after Constantine the mighty Conan,[513] and he was a famous youth most apt to wear the crown, mighty in wars and battle. And he had an uncle who had a [more perfect] claim to the crown [than he], and he, Conan, captured him and slew his two sons. And he, Conan, died in the second year of his reign.[514]

And then ruled Maelgwn,[515] lord of Gwynedd, who was a mighty warrior, the conqueror of many kings - brave, powerful and fearsome. And all his deeds were worthy -or would have been had he not yielded himself up to the sins of Sodom and Gomorrah, for the which he was rendered hateful unto God. But he

---

509) AD 542 seems to be the date that causes most problems for modern scholars concerning the chronology of the historical Arthur. However, it may be significant that the date is not just original to GoM or is something which, it has always been assumed, he invented. It appears in both versions, the Latin and the Old Welsh, both of which claim to be translations of an earlier source book (see note 574).
510) LXI = *Maelgwn Gwynedd*. GoM (11:7) = *Malgo*.
511) As in GoM (11:4). LXI = *Amffidalys*. Amphibalus was, it appears, the name of the Christian priest who hid in Alban's house in Verulamium (today's St Albans). I can find his name only in LXI and GoM. Surprisingly, Bede doesn't name him.
512) GoM (11:4) has the fourth year of his reign.
513) LXI = *Kynan Wledic*. GoM (11:5) = *Aurelius Conanus*.
514) GoM (11:5) states that he died in the third year of his reign.
515) GoM (11:6) states that between the reigns of Aurelius Conanus and Malgo, there fell the reign of one Vortiporius, who is not mentioned in LXI. GoM is right. This king's memorial stone survives.

was the first after Arthur to have subdued the Six Kingdoms to the land of Britain, namely Ireland, Islay, Scotland, the Orkneys, Lochland and Denmark. And these he made subject to the kingdom of Britain. And he died in a monastic church where he beheld the Yellow Spectre[516] through an opening above the church door.

And after him ruled Karedic[517] as king. And he [was a man who] loved war amongst his people. For the which he [also] was [rendered] hateful both unto God and to the Britons. And hearing of it, the Saxons sent envoys to Gormund, a Moorish pirate,[518] who was at that time ravaging Ireland, for he had come with a mighty fleet to conquer that land. And at the behest of the Saxons, this Gormund came to Britain with sixty longships filled with warriors.[519] And in those days the heathen Saxons possessed one part of Britain, whilst the Britons -who were faithful Christians - held the other by lawful right.

And there was bad blood between the Britons and the Saxons. And when Gormund [and his host] had come to aid the Saxons, they [together] made war upon Karedic, defeating him and driving him headlong to Cirencester.[520] And seeing that Gormund had defeated the Britons, [there came] Isembard,[521]

---

516) Maelgwn died in the great plague that swept Europe in the mid-6th century. It began, by all accounts, in Egypt in the year AD 541, reaching Constantinople in 543. It then spread throughout the Roman empire by following the trade routes, sweeping through southern and central Gaul in 544. It reached Britain through trade contacts with Egyptian and other merchantmen involved with the lead-producing industry of Cornwall and the Severn Valley. This plague has been compared with the worst ravages of the Black Death in 1348. Interestingly, although the plague was the common bubonic plague (the Black Death), the Irish annals record that after reaching Ireland in AD 544, the highest mortalities occurred in its aftermath, when it became known as the Yellow Death. The Welsh chronicle here likewise describes the plague as the Yellow Spectre. This phase of the plague helps us to narrow down the year of Maelgwn's death. In this context, Morris (vol. 2, p. 145) states: "...the Irish entry of 551, wrongly interpreted as 547 in the Welsh text" [i.e. the *Annales Cambriae*, which has: '*Mortalitas magna in qua pausat Mailcun rex Guenedotae*' - The great mortality in which died Maelgwn king of Gwynedd] "was there used to date the death of Maelgwn of Gwynedd, and the Saxon Chronicle in turn used the Welsh notice of Maelgwn to give a date to Ida of Northumbria..." From which it seems that Maelgwn died in the year AD 551.
517) As in LXI. GoM (11:8) = *Keredic*.
518) LXI = *Gormwnt brenin Affric*, lit. Gormund, king of Africa. That there never has been a 'king of Africa' is a telling comment upon the insularity of the Briton who first recorded the advent of Gormund. But see note 489. I am aware that the term 'Moorish' strictly speaks of the North African Arabs of the 8th century on, but I have translated the phrase thus because it accurately conveys the type, race, provenance and occupation of the person concerned.
519) GoM (11:8) states that he came with 160,000 Africans.
520) LXI = *ssyssedr* - how ancient the contraction of the name of Cirencester is!
521) LXI = *Imbert*, whom GoM calls the nephew of Louis, king of the Franks.

[erstwhile] king of Gaul, to pay fealty to Gormund and to ask his help in regaining his realm from the hands of his uncle who had deprived him of it. And they came together to Silchester in search of Karedic and to assault the city. And they shut up the citizens within - though nothing did they gain [by that] but a smaller army!

And they held council [together] and devised this plan,[522] to catch a great number of sparrows and tie nutshells to them which are filled with phosphorus. Which birds would then be released to fly onto the thatched roofs of the city. And they did this so that the phosphorous took flame in the air, and in the morning the city was ablaze. And Karedic sallied forth to wage a battle against his foes, but it availed him nothing and he had to take flight across the Severn beyond the borders of Kymry. And straightway Gormund and the Saxons slew [the Britons], burning their cities and castles and sparing none of them alive, layman or clerk. And none of [the Britons] took thought of where there should go, for not even noble descent could save them from the innumerable atrocities of that nation who God had chosen to punish the Britons. And is it any wonder, O wretched people of the land of Britain, that you are so humbled? Your forebears of old did conquer other nations, right down the ages. But you are miserably paying [for your sins], so that you cannot save your own land even from the [Saxon] invader. Poor Britons! Repent your folly, as is just, and take to your hearts these words of God [when He says] in [His] Gospel: "Every kingdom divided against itself shall be desolate, and one house shall fall upon another!" Because it is the disunity of you Britons and your jealousy which have [alone] destroyed this nation. And therefore the wicked heathen [are able to] conquer the heirs to the kingdom!

And when the Saxons had pillaged and burned [the land] and slaughtered [its people] from sea to sea, then Karedic yielded up all Lloegria to them.[523] And those poor [ones who yet lived] dwelt in the furthermost parts of the island towards Cornwall and in the land of Kymry, bearing many assaults from their foes.

And when Teon,[524] archbishop of London, and the archbishop of Eboracum,[525] both witnessed the destruction of the churches, they took up the relics and bones of the saints and fled with them to the most desolate part of

---

522) The following account is entirely omitted from GoM, who (11:8) merely states that: "The city I have mentioned was captured and burnt." This is a significant item of evidence against the supposition that the Welsh chronicle is merely a translation of Geoffrey's Latin *Historia*.
523) GoM (11:10) states that it was Gormund who handed Lloegria to the Saxons.
524) As in LXI = GoM (11:10) = *Theonus*.
525) GoM (11:10) names him as *Tadioceus*.

Snowdon, lest the wretched heathen should lay hold on them [and defile] them. And a great number [of the Britons] fled to Armorica, for nowhere in all Lloegria was there a single church which had escaped destruction at the hands of the heathen Saxons. [Nor was there a place where] learned monks [had not been] slaughtered to a man. And so for many years the Britons lost the sovereignty of the island and all its dominions. And they were governed by three kings, not one, and they fought amongst themselves continually. But neither did the Saxons receive sovereignty of the land, for they also warred amongst themselves and with the Britons also.

And there came [in those days] a certain bishop[526] from Rome to preach amongst the Saxons throughout the land, for they were ignorant of the faith of Christ, which faith they had utterly rooted out from amongst themselves. But for all that, the Britons had kept the faith of Christ undefiled amongst themselves from the days of Eleutherus, bishop of Rome, the very first to send the Christian faith to this land. And he, Augustine, preached amongst the Saxons, but many more laughed him to scorn than believed him. And he came to a sacred high place to which a large crowd followed him, and there, in a great valley, they were in need of water. And there did he, Augustine, pray for water. And an angel came and told him not to fear for his mission, for God would provide him with every necessity. And in that place did a spring [of water] well up out of the ground, and all received water in abundance, and Augustine was gladdened [because of it].[527]

And he went towards Kent where he preached until the king[528] and all his people received the Gospel of Christ. And from thence he went to Riw,[529] and whilst he was preaching there, they, the townspeople, sewed many animals' tails to his cloak to ridicule him. And he prayed that the townspeople [from that day on] should themselves have tails.[530] And from that place he proceeded to London and made enquiry there of the archbishop and the learned clerks whom the Saxons had scattered. And he was told that the archbishop of Caerleon-on-Usk, with seven bishops serving him, was worshipping [God] devoutly, and [that in that place were] also monasteries and sacred choirs in them praising

---

526) i.e. Augustine, who came over in AD 597.
527) Bede, who usually revels in the miraculous, fails to mention this.
528) *Ethelbert*.
529) LXl = *Tre y riw*. GoM omits the place. Given the *riw* element, could it not be Rochester?
530) This account does not appear in Bede. However, Manley Pope (p. 212) states: "This seems to be the real origin of the fabulous tradition, that Kentish men were born with tails; and which in later times was revived, and said by the Papists to have happened to them" [the men of Kent] "at the time of the Reformation."

God and the saints. And [foremost] amongst these was the great monastery of Bangor, [which is] Maelor in the Saxon tongue. And there, not reckoning the priors and servants, were one hundred and twenty monks who lived by the work of their hands. And the abbot of the monastery was Dinawd,[531] and none in his day was more learned than he.

And on seeing this Augustine was glad, and he sent to Dinawd and exhorted him to come and preach [the Gospel] to the Saxons to try to win them to the faith. But Dinawd replied to him that it was not meet that he should preach the faith to such a wicked people as this, who had come from overseas and [who] through treachery and betrayal had murdered our kin and robbed them of their rightful inheritance, [for], "It is not our concern to preach to them, not to serve them, nor [indeed to serve] any man in the land save the archbishop of Caerleon-on-Usk. For he is [the head of our church], the highest [spiritual authority] in the land!"[532]

And when Ethelbert,[533] king of Kent, heard of it, he sent to Ethelfrith,[534] king of Northumbria, and to as many lords as the Saxons possessed [over them], and commanded them straightway to descend upon Dinawd and his monastery, and to heap retribution upon him for his perfidy. And as many of the Saxons as there were in the land, came to Caerleon-on-Usk. And Brochwel, lord of

---

531) GoM (11:12) = *Dinoot*. Bede uses the same spelling. Manley Pope (pp. 212-3) puts an interesting gloss on this episode. He states that the following passage on the massacre of the British Christians has been: "...carefully managed, so as to avoid giving offence to the church of Rome. It tells only what could not be concealed [as does Bede]. The following passage, quoted by Spelman, from an ancient manuscript in the Mostyn collection, gives the speech of Dunod more fully, and whatever be its date, it certainly gives the opinion of the British church truly. 'Know and be assured, that we all jointly and severally, are in humility ready to defer to the Church of God, the Pope of Rome, and every sincere and pious Christian; so to love everyone according to his station, in perfect charity, and to assist them all by word and deed, so that they may become children of God. But as to further deference than this, I know of none, which he whom ye call Pope, or father of father's, can claim or demand. The deference which I have stated, we are ever ready to pay to him, and every Christian. Moreover, we are subject to the Bishop of Caerleon on Uske, who is, under God, our superintendent to keep us in our spiritual path.' In the British Church the bishops were elective. The Gospel of St John was its principal authority. Saints and martyrs were not regarded as intercessors."

532) The earliest argument, it appears, against papal supremacy in Britain and the innovative changes to the Church calendar that Rome had recently introduced through Dionysius Exiguus. Would Geoffrey of Monmouth as a Cistercian monk, or indeed any other author of the 12th century, have dared to invent such an argument, or may we take its existence as a further token of authenticity?

533) LXI = *Edelffled*, an error, it seems, for Ethelbert (see note 534).

534) LXI = *Edelffled*, otherwise Ethelfrid, Saxon king of Northumbria. Bede (1:34) records that he drove the Scots out of England in the year AD 603, the eleventh year of his reign which lasted twenty-four years in total. Ethelfrith thus ruled the Northumbrians from AD 592-616. The massacre at Bangor, occurred in AD 604.

Powis,[535] was lord also of the Kymry, and there were with him a great number of monks from every monastery in those lands held by the Britons, especially from [the great monastery of] Bangor. And they, the warriors of the Britons, gave battle to the Saxons, and Brochwel went to Bangor to summon to him all [the monks of the] Britons. And when Ethelfrith saw such a vast multitude of monks [gathered there], and perceiving that because of them [praying to God] there would be a great slaughter [amongst the Saxons], he commanded that one thousand two hundred of the monks of Bangor should be put to the sword.

And these were the princes of the Kymry who came to Bangor, to Brochwel's aid, namely, Bledric,[536] earl of Cornwall, and Meredith,[537] king of Dyfed, and Kanvan,[538] lord of Gwynedd. And there was a mighty battle between them and the Saxons, in which many were slain on either side. But at the last the Britons won the day, and Ethelfrith was wounded and made to flee, escaping with [the rest of] the Saxons. And the number of Saxon dead was ten thousand and sixty and six. And to the Kymry were lost Bledric, earl of Cornwall, and many with him, for he sustained [the fury of] the battle more than any other man. And all the Kymry rallied together and came to Caerleon-on-Usk.

And in council it was ordained that they should anoint Kadvan, the son of Iago, king over them. And he pursued Ethelfrith and the Saxon host across the Humber. And there did Ethelfrith muster an army and fight with Kadvan. And as their armies closed with each other [for battle], so peace was declared between them upon these conditions, that Ethelfrith should be lord [of all lands] beyond the Humber, and Kadvan [should rule] this side of the Humber. And they bound themselves with hostages to this pact.

And then a quarrel arose between Ethelfrith and his wife over a mistress that he had, and Ethelfrith expelled his wife from the kingdom even though she was with child. And she came to the court of Kadvan and besought him to reconcile [her husband to her]. But Ethelfrith would not be reconciled for all of Kadvan's entreaties. And so the woman remained at the court of Kadvan until she bore a

---

535) LXI = *Brochwel Essgithroc*. GoM (11:13) = *Brochmail*. It is interesting to note that after this battle Roman Catholicism was never able to entirely subjugate the Welsh, in spite of many vicious attempts to do so over the following centuries. It is also interesting to trace the resentment that arose from this massacre, and which was fed by centuries of severe persecution, all the way through the Welsh royal line until it emerged on the throne of England under Henry VIII - himself of Welsh Tudor blood - with devastating and lasting effect for the church of Rome. The massacre at Bangor was all about papal supremacy, as was the Reformation nearly one thousand years later.

536) As in LXI. GoM (11:13) = *Belderic*.

537) LXI = *Mredydd*. GoM (11:13) = *Margodud*.

538) As in LXI. GoM (11:13) = *Cadvan*.

son. And at the same time was a son born to Kadvan's wife. And his name, this son of Kadvan, was Kadwallon,[539] and the name of the son of Ethelfrith was Edwin. And the two boys were raised together until they had grown into young men. And they were sent to Selyf,[540] king of Armorica, to learn protocol and etiquette, horsemanship and the use of weapons. And Selyf rejoiced over them, and they became accomplished exponents of all the manly arts, so that in battle or conflict none were more able than they.

And when Kadvan and Ethelfrith were no more, so each of these boys took his father's place and swore themselves to the same friendship that there had been between their fathers. But when two years had passed, Edwin sought Kadwallon's leave to make himself a crown which he could wear when he celebrated the holy days beyond the Humber, in accordance with the privileges enjoyed by their forebears. And it was ordained that the wise counsellors of that region should debate the matter on the banks of the river Douglas.

And in that place did Kadwallon rest his head upon the knee of Brian, the son of Nefyn, his nephew. And Brian [who was surnamed] Longfellow,[541] wept, and the tears fell upon Kadwallon's face so that he awoke, thinking that it was raining. And the king asked Brian the cause of his weeping. And he, Brian, replied, "The Britons shall have much cause to weep from this day on, for you have yielded up the highest dignity that you or the nation possessed, even that thing which had been our greatest symbol of office from the days of Maelgwn, [lord of] Gwynedd, until now. [And you have done this thing] by granting to the lying, treacherous, oath-breaking Saxons the authority to anoint their own kings. And so will they come together and by lies and deceit shall overcome the whole island of Britain. For this cause it would have been better for you to have oppressed them rather than exalt them. How can you not recall, my lord, what they did to Vortigern, the first [of our people] to hold concourse with them rather than [with] honest men? [And] for the good [that he did them], they repaid him [with] evil. After which things they betrayed the mighty Ambrosius and poisoned him, and Uther Pendragon with him! And they broke vows by promising allegiance to Mordred against Arthur, and in the latter days did they entice Gormund to lay waste Karedic's kingdom, and banished him in disgrace from [his own] realm!"

And when Brian had spoken these words, Kadwallon sent envoys to Edwin to tell him that the council would not allow any crown [to be worn] in the land of Britain save the crown of London. But Edwin replied that he would

---

539) As in LXI. GoM (12:1) = Cadwallo.
540) LXI = sselyf. GoM (12:1) = Salomon.
541) LXI = Braint hir, lit. Brian the Long or Tall.

[nonetheless] have a crown, however much this may displease Kadwallon. And Kadwallon told him that if he did as much, then he, Kadwallon, would have the head which wore that crown chopped off!

And from that day forth there was a quarrel between them, and each mustered the greatest army that he could, and there was a great battle between them. And Edwin was victorious, and he drove Kadwallon headlong into Ireland. And Edwin achieved sovereignty by slaughtering and laying waste [the land] throughout Kadwallon's domains. And wherever he, Kadwallon, sought to come ashore, then at that place to resist him was Edwin and all his host. And this was through the counsel of one Pellitus,[542] an astrologer who could foretell all things for the Saxon king by the flight of birds and [by] the stars.

And on seeing this, Kadwallon lost all hope, for he thought that he could never recover his realm. And so he went forth to Selyf, king of Armorica, to lament his ill fortune and to ask his help and counsel in restoring his kingdom [to him]. And as he was sailing with his fleet towards Armorica, there blew an adverse wind and all his ships were scattered one from another. And Kadwallon was seasick so that for three days and nights he could neither eat nor drink. But on the fourth day he was well again, and the moment a favourable wind arose, they set sail towards Armorica.[543]

And Selyf rejoiced over them and kindly undertook to help Kadwallon, for it was most grievous for him to see that a heathen invader could oppress the Britons so shamefully. And he was amazed at the faint-heartedness of the Britons against the Saxons, whom every other nation has fought off but theirs, saying, "For since [the time in which] the mighty Maximianus and Conan Mairiadawc first arrived in Armorica with all the nobility of Britain, no man has been able, from then until now, to maintain the sovereignty of the land of Britain. And I grieve therefore that I cannot myself wreak vengeance upon the Saxons."

And Kadwallon was greatly abashed at the words of Selyf, but he thanked him for his kindness and spoke these words to him, "Think it no strange matter, my lord, that the people were despondent who remained in the land of Britain, for there was left amongst them not one of noble blood who had not come to this place with Conan Mairiadawc. And when the kingdom fell into the hands of the ignoble, the indolent and the mindless, they could neither govern nor keep it, for they had given themselves up to gluttony, drunkenness, greed and arrogance. As Gildas says, familiarity with sin degrades the people until judgment

---

542) As in GoM (12:4). LXI = *Pelidys*.
543) At this point, GoM (12:4) inserts the story of Brian, who, failing to find food for the king, cooked for him a piece of his own flesh.

falls upon them, because they sought no remedy from [the only One who could help them], the truest Physician of all.[544] And therefore, my lord, it is not to be wondered at that they are loathsome in God's eyes, and that He has put a foreign oppressor over them to lay them low in judgment for their sin. But for this cause I came, my lord, to beg your help. For Maelgwn, [lord of] Gwynedd, who was the fourth to reign after Arthur over the entire kingdom of Britain, had two sons, Einion[545] and Run.[546] The son of Run was Beli, whose son was Iago, whose son was Kadvan, my father. And Run, after the death of his brother, Einion, and after his revenge upon the Saxons, gave his daughter's hand in marriage to the younger Howel, son of Ambrosius of Armorica, the same who with Arthur conquered many nations. And the younger Howel had a son through his wife, whom he named Alan. And this Alan's son was your own father, a powerful and a mighty man!"

And Kadwallon remained in Armorica for that winter, and was urged in council to send Brian Longfellow to the land of Britain, there to make enquiry concerning Pellitus, the astrologer of Edwin the king, and of the Saxons. And so came Brian to the land of Britain[547] in the guise of a pilgrim carrying an iron cross[548] in his hand. And he came to Edwin's court at Eboracum, and as Brian was mingling amongst the poor, he saw his sister[549] carrying a dish in which to fetch water for the queen to wash in. And the girl told Brian of the ways of the court and about the astrologer. And at the time when the astrologer came out to distribute alms amongst the poor, Brian ran him through with the iron cross so that he fell dead to the earth. And none knew who had slain him.

And afterwards he went to Exeter and summoned to him many of the Britons there. And he fortified the city and the castle, and told them [plainly] who had slain the astrologer. And he sent tidings to Kadwallon [of what had come to pass], and urged him to come to Britain as soon as he could. And [he told him] that he would muster all the Britons [together] for when he arrived there.

---

544) See Gildas chap. 21.
545) As in LXI. GoM (12:6) = *Ennianus*.
546) As in LXI and GoM (12:6).
547) GoM (12:7) states that he landed at Southampton.
548) Although Jones (1929) translates this as 'crutch', an iron cross is a better rendering. The Latin word *cruce* (cross) was often transposed into 'crutch.' An example is the medieval monastic brotherhood of the Crutched Friars, who wore a large cross on the front of their habits. GoM (12:7) merely states that it was an iron rod or staff.
549) GoM (12:7) adds that Edwin (AD 616-33) had carried her off from Worcester.

And when Penda,[550] the Saxon prince, had heard of it, he came with a great army and surrounded the city of Exeter. And on receiving news of this, Kadwallon came to Britain with ten thousand mounted knights given him in aid by Selyf, king of Armorica. And he stayed not until he came Exeter, and there he divided his army into four legions and waged war upon the Saxons, slaying multitudes of them and capturing Penda. And to save his life, Penda paid fealty to Kadwallon, siding with him against the Saxons and giving hostages [for his pledge] that he would remain loyal to the king.

And Kadwallon marched through Northumbria [until he encountered Edwin]. And he, Edwin, descended with his Saxon army upon Kadwallon, and there was Edwin slain along with Godbold,[551] lord of the Orkneys, and all the host. And when Kadwallon had won the day, he began to slaughter the Saxons by sword and fire. And he slew women by having their unborn infants ripped from their bellies, hoping to eliminate the Saxon [name] from the land. And in that place were slain king Offric,[552] his two nephews, and Eadan,[553] lord of the Scots, who had come to Offric's aid. And all his host were slain with him.

And in his, Edwin's, stead was Oswald[554] made king [over the Saxons]. And Kadwallon pursued him [relentlessly] from place to place. And Oswald sought refuge beyond the wall which Severus, emperor of Rome, had built between Deira and Bernicia. And Kadwallon sent Penda with the greater part of his army to give him chase, and Penda cornered him in a field called Hevenfield.[555] And Oswald raised up the image of the cross, and said to his comrades, "Let us beseech Almighty God upon our knees and pray with all our hearts that He will deliver us from the evil Penda, for God knows that we fight to set our people free!"

And the following day did Oswald, trusting in God, assault his enemies. And he won the day.

---

550) Penda of Mercia, the renowned pagan king. According to the *Anglo-Saxon Chronicle*, he ruled from AD 626-56.

551) As in GoM (12:8). LXI = *gorblod*.

552) As in LXI. GoM (12:8) = *Offrid*. GoM states (with Bede) that *Offric* was the son of Edwin (AD 616-33). Bede renders the name *Osfrid*.

553) As in GoM (12:9). LXI = *Pyanda*. I have adopted GoM's rendering here to avoid confusion with the Saxon *Penda*.

554) As in GoM (12:10). LXI = *Osswall*. Oswald reigned AD 632-642.

555) As in GoM (12:10). LXI = *maes nefawl*, lit. the Heavenly Field. Bede (3:2) = *Hefenfelth*. The battle took place, according to the *Anglo-Saxon Chronicle*, on 14th October AD 633.

But as soon as Kadwallon knew of it, he pursued him to Burne[556] and defeated him there. And in that place did Penda slay Oswald the king.

And after Oswald was slain, Oswy, [surnamed] Whitebrow,[557] his brother, was anointed king in his stead. And he collected money and sent it to Kadwallon - for he was high king over all the land - and Oswy paid fealty to him. But then arose his two nephews, his brother's sons, to wage war upon Oswy, though it availed them nothing and they made their peace with him. And Oswy made overtures to Penda, king of Mercia, to seek his help in making war upon Kadwallon. But Penda told him that whilst he breathed he would in no wise disavow his fealty to the king without cause.

And the following Whitsuntide, Kadwallon held court at London, and to that place came all the nobility, [both] Briton and Saxon, to Kadwallon, save Oswy the Whitebrow. And Penda asked the king why Oswy had not come. And the king replied, "Because he is unwell."

"Truly that is not so," said Penda, "[for] he asked me to join myself to him in his intent to wreak vengeance upon you for his brother['s death]. And because I would not consent to this, he had envoys sent to Germany to ask the Saxons [there] to help him avenge his brother upon both you and me also. And in token of these things, he has exiled his two nephews from the land and has sought an alliance with me against you. And thus he destroys the peace of the realm. Give me leave, my lord, either to slay him or drive him from these shores."

And so Kadwallon held council [concerning these things]. And Meredith, lord of Dyfed, said to him, "You should not have failed in your first resolve, namely to expel every Saxon from this land. Therefore, grant Penda leave to wage war upon Oswy, that the two of them, [Saxons both], might be slain, for oath-breakers may look for no reward [for their pains] but [that of] utter destruction!"

And Kadwallon granted Penda leave to wage war upon Oswy, and Penda pursued Oswy beyond the Humber, and amidst [great] slaughter began to set ablaze his kingdom. And Oswy offered Penda a mighty sum in treasure to buy peace, but he, Penda, would not accept it and warred [yet] against him. And Oswy committed the outcome to God and Penda was slain in the first

---

556) As in GoM (12:10). LXI = *Byrnwy*. Bede (3:2) = *Deniseburn*. Rowley Water in Northumberland, and Bourne in Lincolnshire are both thought to be candidates for the site. But as Griscom (p. 547) points out, it is clear upon comparison that Geoffrey of Monmouth did not borrow the name from Bede, as is often assumed.
557) LXI = *Osswyd Aelwynn*. GoM (12:11) = *Oswi*. Oswy reigned AD 642-71.

encounter.[558]

And Kadwallon granted to Penda's son, Wulfhere,[559] the kingdom [of Mercia in Penda's place]. And he, Wulfhere, waged war upon Edbart,[560] a prince of Mercia.[561] But at last Kadwallon reconciled them. And Kadwallon reigned over the land of Britain for forty-eight years as high king over the Kymry and Lloegria. And on the fifteenth day of December he fell sick and died. And the Kymry anointed his body with rare ointments and placed it inside a copper likeness [of himself] made with wondrous craftsmanship. And this figure they placed upon a copper horse over a gate of London, that it might [seem to] sally forth against the Saxon. And at this gate there was built a church dedicated to the name of God and St Martin.[562] And [in that church] were masses sung for the soul of Kadwallon, the one of whom Merlin prophesied as the Brazen Horseman.[563] And afterwards did Kadwallader, [surnamed] the Blessed,[564] become king. And the year of Christ was....[565]

And Kadwallader ruled the land in peace for eleven years, and he fell ill with a lingering sickness. And strife arose amongst the Kymry, for Kadwallader's mother had been a sister on her father's side to Penda, her mother being born of a noble family of north Kymry. And when Kadwallon had made peace with Penda, he had taken to wife she who was to become Kadwallader's mother. Now while this strife was raging, there came a plague and famine[566]upon the Britons as God's punishment for their sins. And over all the land of Britain there was not to be found a mouthful of food, save the meat of wild animals. And those who lived could not bury those who had died in the

---

558) According to GoM (12:13), the battle took place on the banks of the river *Wunued*, the present-day Are in Yorkshire.

559) LXI = *Wlvryd*. GoM (12:13) = *Wulfred*.

560) As in LXI. GoM (12:13) = *Edbert*. GoM states that the alliance was made with *Edbert* and *Eba*, two Mercian nobles.

561) As in GoM (12:13).

562) The gate must have been Cripplegate, one of the oldest in London's wall, near to which the college of St Martins le Grand was built.

563) Merlin's prophecy of the *Brazen Horseman* is not found in GoM.

564) LXI = *Kydwaladr Vendigaid*. GoM (12:14) = *Cadwallader*.

565) According to the *Brut y Tywysogyon* (The Chronicle of the Princes - Peniarth MS 20), Cadwallader died on 12th May AD 682. Given that LXI goes on to tell us that he reigned eleven years, then the missing date here must be AD 671.

566) *The Anglo-Saxon Chronicle* records this plague under the year AD 664. The plague continued to rage for several decades. Intriguingly, though it decimated the Britons, the Saxons in England barely noticed it because of the Britons' refusal to have any contact with them (see Morris. vol. 2. pp. 222-4).

famine, [for such was the multitude of the dead and the weakness of those who lived]. And they who were able to go to other lands, did so, saying, "Truly, Lord, you have given us up as sheep to be devoured by wolves!"

And Kadwallader commanded that a fleet be made ready for himself that he might go to Armorica, saying, "Alas to us sinners, for by the multitude of our iniquities have we offended against God. There had been a time when we [might have ceased from our sins and] turned to God. But we did it not, and so God takes from us our inheritance, which neither the Romans nor any other could do - but He!"

And so with weeping did Kadwallader go to Alan, king of Armorica, and he, Alan, rejoiced to see him. And in Britain, through plague and famine, there were left alive only those who had gone into the wilderness to hunt wild animals. And the plague [ravaged the land] for eleven years, and the Saxons sent to Germany saying that the land of Britain now lay undefended, and to come and take it freely to themselves. And so they gathered great multitudes of men and women and landed in the north. And they settled the land from Lochland to Cornwall, for there were no Britons left [who might] oppose them. And from that day the [few] Britons [who remained] lost the sovereignty of the island of Britain.

And after these things, Kadwallader besought Alan to come with him to win back the land of Britain from the pagan Saxons who had overrun it. But there spoke an angel to Kadwallader, saying that he was not to return to the land of Britain, for it was not God's pleasure that the Britons should return there until the times be fulfilled that were spoken of by Merlin in the presence of Vortigern. And the angel commanded Kadwallader to go to Rome, there to submit his body to penance that he might be counted amongst the saints. And the angel said to him that because of his own merits and good works, the Britons would rule the second time in the land of Britain when the times set by God had been fulfilled, "which shall not be until your bones are carried from Rome to Britain. And that will be when the bones of all the saints are revealed again as [they were] in former times, before they were hidden for fear of the Saracens.[567]

---

567) LXI = *ssarssiniait*. As Griscom (pp. 547-8) tells us: "This is a curious native prophecy growing out of an historic event. Geoffrey [of Monmouth] uses the term *paganorum*; but the Welsh uses *ssarssiniait*, or 'saracens'. According to the *Liber Pontificalis*...in 846, Adelvertus, Count of Tuscany and Protector of Corsica, sent a letter to Pope Sergius II, warning him of an approaching attack by the Saracens, and urging that the treasures accumulated at the Basilicas outside the walls, where the bodies of Sts. Peter and Paul were deposited, be removed to safety within the fortifications. This was not done, the Saracens were victorious, took the Basilicas and immense booty, and directed their fury against the tombs of the Apostles..."

And when this time comes to pass, so the Britons shall win again the possession and governance of the land of Britain."

And Kadwallader came before Alan, king of Armorica, and revealed all these things to him. And Alan took the books of Merlin and the prophecies of the Sybil, to see whether they agreed with the words of the angel [or no]. And when he found the prophecies, he thought it good to counsel Kadwallader to go to Rome.

And Kadwallader sent Yvor, his son, and Ynyr, his nephew,[568] to maintain the allegiance of the Britons toward their lawful king, lest the people of Kymry should be scattered. And Kadwallader renounced all earthly things for the love of God and went to Rome to do penance. And on the twelfth day of December he died, his soul entering [the Kingdom of] Heaven in the six hundred and eighty-eighth year from the nativity of Christ.[569]

And Yvor, son of Kadwallader, and Ynyr, his nephew, mustered a mighty army and brought them to the land of Britain where they waged war against the Saxons for twenty-eight years.[570] But it availed them nothing, for the plague had carried off so many of the Britons that they could not expel the foreign invader. And from that day forth they were no longer called Britons - but Welsh!

And the Saxons prudently maintained peace between themselves, and they built towns and castles, and in this way they threw off the sovereignty of the Britons. And they possessed all Lloegria under [the kingship of] Athelstan,[571] the first of the Saxon kings to wear a crown in the land. And from that day did the native people of the land lose their name and could not retrieve it, enduring

---

568) As in LXI and GoM (12:18).
569) According to the *Brut y Tywysogyon*, he died in AD 682.
570) GoM (12:18) has seventy-nine years, which implies further illegibility in the source book.
571) LXI = *Edelstan*. GoM (12:18) = *Adelstan*. Athelstan reign AD 924-39. This remarkable jump forward in time of some 250 years, is simply to inform the reader of the period in which Britons finally gave up all hope of repossessing the land.

without respite the oppression of the Saxons.[572] But the princes who did rule over the Kymry, one after another....[573]

I, Walter of Oxford, translated this book
from Welsh into Latin, and in my old age
have translated it again from
Latin into Welsh.[574]

Here ends the Chronicle of the Britons.

---

572) The following most informative explicit appears at this point in both the Berne and Harlech manuscripts of Geoffrey of Monmouth's Latin *Historia*, which was made from the same source material as the Welsh chronicle. Thorpe (p. 284) translates it thus: "The Welsh, once they had degenerated from the noble state enjoyed by the Britons, never afterwards recovered the overlordship of the island. On the contrary, they went on quarrelling with the Saxons and among themselves and remained in a state of either civil or external war. The task of describing their kings, who succeeded from that moment onwards in Wales, I leave to my contemporary, Caradoc of Llancarfan. The kings of the Saxons I leave to William of Malmesbury and Henry of Huntingdon. I recommend these last to say nothing at all about the kings of the Britons, seeing that they do not have in their possession the book in the British language which Walter, Archdeacon of Oxford, brought from Wales (see note 574). It is this book which I have been at such pains to translate into Latin in this way, for it was composed with great accuracy about the doings of these princes and in their honour." - Caradoc of Llancarfan is known to us as the compiler of the *Brut y Tywysogyon*, or *Chronicle of the Princes*, which directly follows on from the *Brut y Britanniait*.

573) The *Brut y Tywysogyon* continues the story from this point. An English translation by Thomas Jones, complete with the Welsh text, was published by the University of Wales Press of Cardiff in 1955.

574) This colophon, written by Walter of Oxford, which appears on folio 135v. of our chronicle, *Jesus Coll. MS LXI*, is one of the most telling items of evidence against the modern supposition that Geoffrey of Monmouth's claim to have translated an original book is an invention on his part. Conversely, in support of the colophon's statement, Geoffrey of Monmouth makes no mention of a Welsh translation of the chronicle, simply because, as the colophon here tells us, that translation was made only after he had completed his Latin translation. It is, however, obvious when comparing Geoffrey's *Historia* with the Welsh chronicle, that the Welsh is not in fact a straightforward translation of Geoffrey's Latin as is often supposed and as the colophon would imply if interpreted too literally. It omits material that Geoffrey includes - *Merlin's Prophecies*, for example - and includes items that Geoffrey omits - the story of *Llefelys*, for instance. Moreover, Geoffrey often takes licence to fill out his narrative with speeches and so on, which may or may not have been copied from other sources, but which are entirely absent in the Welsh chronicle. In other words, it would appear from Geoffrey's additions that *Jesus Coll. MS LXI* is a lot closer to the contents of the original source book than is Geoffrey's Latin version.

Appendix I - Family tree of Ygerna (Eigr)

(Referenced from footnote 398)

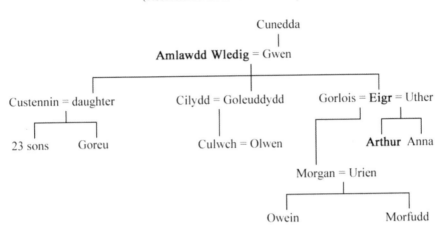

Appendix II - After the Flood

For further discussion of issues related to this document, see the following chapters of *After the Flood*.

Chapter 3 Nennius and the Table of European Nations
Chapter 4 The Chronicles of the early Britons
Chapter 5 The History of the early British Kings
Chapter 6 The Descent of the Anglo-Saxon Kings
Chapter 7 The Descent of the Danish and Norwegian Kings
Chapter 8 The Descent of the Irish Celtic Kings
Appendix 4 Surviving MSS of the early Welsh Chronicles
Appendix 5 The Latin Text of Nennius 17 and 18
Appendix 6 The Molmutine Laws and Pagan Britain
Appendix 7 The Genealogy of the early British Kings
Appendix 8 The Descent of the East Saxon Kings

Bibliography

Ashe, C. 1990. *Mythology of the British Isles*. Methuen. London.

Bede. See Sherley-Price.

Bradford. *Guide to the Greek Islands*. Collins. London.

Cooper, Bill. 2017. *After the Flood*. 2nd edition. CSM. Portsmouth.

Flinders Petrie, W.M. 1917. 'Neglected British History.' Proc. Brit. Academy. Vol. VIII. pp. 128.

Goeffrey of Monmouth. See Griscom, Thompson and Thorpe.

Gildas. See Morris.

Griscom, Acton. 1929. *Geoffrey of Monmouth's Historia Regum Britanniae*. Longman, Green & Co. London.

Jones, Canon Robert Ellis. 1929. 'Untitled Literal Translation of Jesus College MS LXI (now at the Bodleian Library, Oxford).' See Griscom pp. 217-536.

Manley Pope. 1862. *A History of the Kings of Ancient Britain*. Simpkin, Marshall & Co. London.

Morris, John. 1978. *Gildas: The Ruin of Britain: and other documents; Arthurian Period Sources*, Volume 7. Phillimore, Chichester.

Probert, W. 1823. *Ancient Laws of Cambria*. London.

Roberts, Peter. 1811. *Chronicle of the Kings*. (Sole remaining copy held at Bodleian Library.

Shelfmark Douce T., 301). A facsimile reprint, excluding the notes and dissertations, is available from Llanerch Press under the title: *The Chronicle of the Kings of Britain: translated from the Welsh copy attributed to Tysilio.*

Séllincourt, Aubrey de. 1960. Livy: *The Early History of Rome*. Penguin Classics. London.

Sherley-Price, Leo. 1985. Bede: *A History of the English Church and People*. Dorset Press.

New York. Also available in Penguin Classics.

Stowe, John. 1614. *The Annales or Generall Chronicle of England*. Thomas Adams. London. (Copy held at Croydon Reference Library).

Tatlock, J.. P. 1950. *The Legendary History of Britain: Geoffrey of Monmouth 's Historia Regum Britanniae and its EarlyVernacular Versions*. Univ. Calif. Press.

Thompson, Aaron. 1718. *The British History Translated into English from the Latin of Geoffrey of Monmouth*. London (Guildhall Hall Library).

Thorpe, Lewis. 1966. *Geoffrey of Monmouth: The History of the Kings of Britain*. Penguin Classics. London.

Thorpe, Lewis. tr. 1974. *Gregory of Tours: The History of the Franks*. Penguin Classics. London.

Wade-Evans, A.W. 1938. *Nennius' History of the Britons*. SPCK.

West, David. 1990. Virgil: *The Aeneid*. Penguin Classics. London.

Westwood, Jennifer. 1985. *Albion: A Guide to Legendary Britain*. Granada. London.

Further publications by Bill Cooper available from CSM

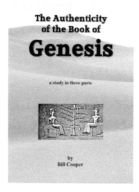

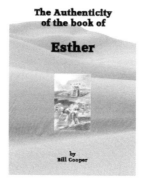

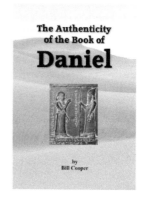

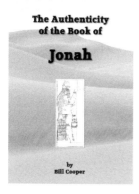

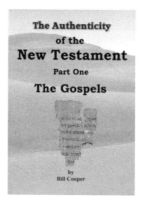

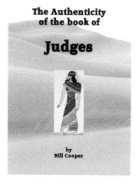

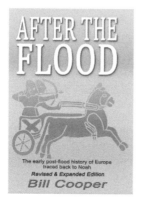

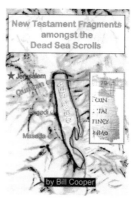

The Authenticity
of the Book of

Joshua

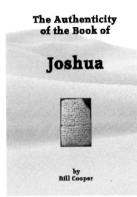

by
Bill Cooper

The Authenticity
of the

New Testament

Part 2: Acts, The Epistles
& Revelation

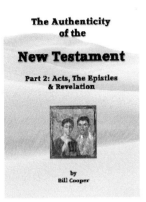

by
Bill Cooper